■SCHOLASTIC

Inclusive Practice
in the Early Years

Speech and Language Difficulties

Supporting Special Needs in the Early Years Foundation Stage

▲ ● ■

Ages
3–5

Dr Hannah Mortimer

Author
Dr Hannah Mortimer

Editor
Sally Gray

Series Designer
Rebecca Male

Designer
Q2A Media

Illustrations
Debbie Clark

Cover artwork
Rebecca Male

Acknowledgements

Cover artwork © Comstock Inc.; Corel Corporation; Digitalstock/Corbis; Ingram Publishing; Jupiter Images; Photodisc Inc/Getty; Stockbyte.
Every effort has been made to trace copyright holders and the publishers apologise for any inadvertent omissions.

Text © 2007, Hannah Mortimer
© 2007, Scholastic Ltd

Designed using Adobe InDesign

Published by Scholastic Ltd, Villiers House,
Clarendon Avenue, Leamington Spa, Warwickshire CV32 5PR

Visit our website at www.scholastic.co.uk

Printed by Bell and Bain Ltd, Glasgow

2 3 4 5 6 7 8 9 0   9 0 1 2 3 4 5 6

British Library Cataloguing-in-Publication Data A catalogue record for this book is available from the British Library.

ISBN 978-0439-94564-6

Mixed Sources
Product group from well-managed
forests and other controlled sources
www.fsc.org Cert no. TT-COC-002769
© 1996 Forest Stewardship Council

FSC

Speech and Language Difficulties

Introduction

▲●■ New developments

This new series *Inclusive Practice in Early Years* aims to bring you up to date with what you need to know in order to plan inclusive practice for the children you work with who have special educational needs (SEN) within the Early Years Foundation Stage (EYFS). It builds on the successful *Special Needs in Early Years* Series (Scholastic) in which readers were introduced to their duties under the SEN Code of Practice. In the original series, readers were shown how to plan activities that contributed towards the Early Learning Goals for all the children and yet which also carried specifically targeted learning outcomes for children who have SEN. In this new series the activities are linked to the EYFS and therefore cover a broader age range from zero to five years. The activity sheets are open-ended so that all colleagues can follow a child's 'play plan' when interacting and supporting a child with a given area of need. This approach is less prescriptive and helps you to tune into the child's needs and use general strategies for supporting all of the child's play and learning, planned or otherwise.

The more open-ended approach means that you will find the book a flexible resource for encouraging all children's early language development, meaning that it will be helpful for SureStart services and Children's Centres as well as early years settings.

▲●■ About this series

There is a handbook that accompanies this Series, the *Inclusive Practice Handbook*, which covers all the basic information that you need to know in order to apply the SEN Code of Practice to your setting. Though the Code has not changed since the previous series, there is now new terminology and a greater emphasis on inclusion and disability awareness. This handbook will bring you up to date on the recent changes and help you to see special educational needs in terms of removing barriers and personalising your teaching. There are also activity books on supporting these areas of special need in the EYFS:

• Behavioural, Emotional and Social Difficulties
• Autistic Spectrum Disorder
• Speech and Language Difficulties

▲●■ Aims of this book

This book will be of most use to you if used flexibly and dipped into. The aim of this book is to tune you into the particular barriers faced in the EYFS by children who have speech and language difficulties, providing you with a range of ideas that will help you to plan how to change what you provide in order to include these children fully. Inclusion in its widest sense is a process of identifying, understanding and breaking down barriers to participation and belonging (this definition was published by the Early Childhood Forum in 2003).

The activity pages in this new series come in the form of open-ended 'play plans'. Each is focused on an area of play and learning in which a child with speech and language difficulties is likely to face particular barriers, and each plan is linked to the EYFS framework. Play plans can be photocopied, adapted and displayed for staff members to refer to on a daily basis.

▲ ● ■ How the book is organised

At the beginning of the book are two chapters to introduce you to this particular area of special educational need. In the first you meet the children concerned and find out how to recognise the children who might need additional support. What are speech and language difficulties and how do they affect a child's development and communication? Why is early intervention so important? How do the various conditions and difficulties overlap? The next chapter helps you to understand some of the barriers faced by these children in the EYFS and how you can plan support. In order to meet these children's needs inclusively, it is important for settings to change, rather than expect sudden changes in the children concerned. The thread of this book is to adopt a social model to the learning difficulty rather than a medical model – your role is not to 'fix' something that is wrong within the child, but to identify barriers and personalise learning so that they can participate fully.

▲ ● ■ The activity chapters

There then follow six activity chapters, each focusing on an area of the EYFS where children with speech and language difficulties face the most barriers. We have chosen to focus on these six areas:

These have been chosen because of the difficulties and differences children with

Focus:	Area of learning:
Language for Communication	CLL
Language for Thinking	CLL
Linking Sounds and Letters	CLL
Responding to Experiences	CD
Expressing and Communicating Ideas	CD
Developing Imagination and Imaginative Play	CD

speech and language difficulties may have in developing language and speech, using language in their thinking and imagination and developing confidence in expressing their ideas to others. Though the children's difficulties are not confined to these six focus areas, you should develop enough ideas throughout the book to become sensitive to their needs in other areas so that you can plan your own interventions when appropriate. You will find photocopiable forms and some useful references, resources and organisations listed at the end of the book.

▲ ● ■ Using the assessment sheets

All effective planning flows from assessment and observation and is subject to monitoring and evaluation. At the beginning of each activity chapter you will find a general introduction to that particular focus of play followed by an assessment sheet. This photocopiable sheet allows you to observe and record what a child with speech and language difficulties can do at the moment in terms of their development within the EYFS framework. Use or adapt these sheets flexibly in the light of what you know about a particular child's needs – each child's pathway to language will be individual and unique. There will clearly be skills that the child demonstrates almost all of the time, others that are demonstrated sometimes (depending on the child's mood and the particular context of the day) and others still where the child has not demonstrated that skill or learning behaviour at all. This 'always/sometimes/never' recording method enables you to make a very simple assessment of the starting points for your teaching and support, concentrating on behaviours that the child demonstrates sometimes, though not always. By starting your interventions at the level of 'emergent skills', both you and the child concerned have a greater chance of success and progress.

▲ ● ■ Using the play plans

Six of the skills or competencies on each assessment sheet have been asterisked and correspond to 'play plans' that can be adapted and used with the child to support that skill or competency. In this way, you are using the assessment to identify starting points for teaching and support and then selecting a plan that will help you all get started. Some of the play plans can be dipped into in any order to suit your circumstances and some need to be followed in a specific order – those that can be dipped into are clearly marked with a 'Dip-In' icon. **Dip in** Sequential plans are numbered in the order of the sequence. Each play plan is written in general terms and may be adapted or used as a springboard for developing your own more personalised plan, depending on the needs of the particular child. For this purpose

there is a blank template at the back of the book (page). There are also blank spaces within the existing plans to develop your own personalised approaches.

The play plans start from a very early stage of development so that you can use them for babies deemed to be 'at risk' of delayed language development as well as those already identified as having SEN.

▲ ● ■ Monitoring progress

Highlight interventions on the play plans if you wish to make them a particular focus, or use dating and initials to record who has applied each intervention and when. You will find a monitoring sheet on page 86 to help you record how your play plan went; what you did, how it worked and what you plan to go on to next. There is also a summary sheet on page 88 to help you record all the interventions that you have been working on ready for review meetings and this will also help you all to plan the child's next individual education plan (IEP). There is further information about SEN monitoring in line with the SEN Code of Practice in the Inclusive Practice Handbook also in this series. Monitoring sheets are an excellent way to share progress with parents and carers and you can use the assessment/play plan/monitoring framework as a useful way of involving the family in your interventions. Outside professionals should recognise the steps that you are working through on your assessment sheets and can provide you with more specific and personalised advice if the child you are working with has more specialist needs.

▲ ● ■ Reflective practice

In each activity chapter, you will find ideas for how you can observe (using the 'look, listen and note' format) and how you can plan effective practice. This way of thinking should already be familiar to you through your knowledge of EYFS. However, you might not have had previous experience of applying the principles to children who have speech and language difficulties and the ideas in each activity chapter will show you how to do this. Reflective practice involves thinking carefully about what you are doing and adjusting what you do in the light of your findings. In order to do this in your work with children with speech and language difficulties, you will need to tune in to what these difficulties mean for the children and for your practice, learn how you can plan approaches based on your discoveries and then evaluate how effective your interventions have been. We hope that you find the format suggested in this series easy to use, effective for the children concerned and a helpful way of developing your reflective practice.

▲ ● ■ Working with others

Find out who else is available in your authority for advising you when you work with children with speech and language difficulties. Your local Children's Services department (special educational needs/inclusion section) or Speech and Language Therapy Service should be able to advise you. Remember too that the real experts are the parents and carers themselves. Take time right at the beginning of your relationship together to let them tell their story and share their interpretation of their child. If the Early Support materials (see page 8) are used in your area, then parents will have a folder full of information that they can share with you from the start. You will read more about working with others in the Inclusive Practice Handbook. Remember, that when using paperwork and other communications with parents and carers, it is important to ascertain if there are any translation or literacy concerns to be addressed.

Useful organisations and websites

Organisations

- ACE Centres – information and advice on augmentative and alternative communication aids and equipment. www.ace-north.org.uk and www.ace-centre.org.uk (for the south)
- Afasic – a UK charity to help children affected by speech, language and communication impairments. Helpline: 08453 555577, www.afasic.org.uk
- Association of Speech and Language Therapists in Independent Practice (ASLTIP). Tel: 0870 2413357, www.asltip.co.uk
- The British Stammering Association (BSA). Tel: 020 8983 1003, www.stammering.org
- Cleft Lip and Palate Association (CLAPA). Tel: 020 7833 4883, www.clapa.com
- The Dyspraxia Foundation – for advice and resources on developmental dyspraxia and speech dyspraxia. Helpline: 01462 454 986, www.dyspraxiafoundation.org.uk
- Early Support – the Early Support Programme relates to disabled children aged 0-5 years and publishes various support booklets. They include booklets for parents on a range of conditions including Speech and Language Difficulties and Autistic Spectrum Disorders as well as a comprehensive Family Pack. www.earlysupport.org.uk
- The Hanen Centre (parent training and publications on the Hanen approach to language and communication) www.hanen.org
- I CAN – a charity that helps children to communicate. They produce useful resources, run some specialist provision and also organise training. Tel: 0845 225 4071, www.ican.org.uk
- Makaton Vocabulary Development Project (information about Makaton sign vocabulary and training): 31 Firwood Drive, Camberley, Surrey GU15 3QB. Tel: 01276 61390, www.makaton.org
- The National Autistic Society, 393 City Road, London EC1V 1NG. Helpline: 0845 070 4004. www.nas.org.uk, e-mail: autismhelpline@nas.org.uk
- The Royal College of Speech and Language Therapists. Tel: 020 7378 1200, www.rcslt.org
- Selective Mutism Information and Research Association (SMIRA). Tel: 0116 2127411

Websites

- Bilingualism - www.bilingualism.co.uk
- British Sign Language – www.britishsignlanguage.com (to download live performances of signs)
- PECS (Picture Exchange Communication System) – www.pecs.org.uk
- Signalong – signing and singing – www.signalong.org.uk
- Talking Point: information from I CAN on communication development and disability – www.talkingpoint.org.uk
- Writing with symbols/Widgit – www.widgit.com

Meet the Children

Speech and language difficulties occur for many different reasons and in this chapter you will be introduced to what they mean for the children concerned.

▲ ● ■ Dillan

Dillan is three and is keen to communicate and loves coming to nursery. He talks very quickly and it is not always possible to hear what he is saying as most of his words seem to be full of vowels and just a few consonants. Fortunately, this is not getting in the way of Dillan joining in the activities of the group. However, his lack of clarity means that the adults cannot be sure just how much he is understanding and how his thinking skills are developing. He has now been referred to a speech and language therapist who is providing exercises for him to do at home. He has also been fitted with grommets to improve his hearing.

▲ ● ■ Jonathan

Jonathan is four and first came to the staff's attention because of his challenging behaviour. He seemed to get very angry very quickly and this seemed to be linked to frustration. He did not follow instructions and was upset as soon as situations did not go his own way. After careful observation, staff realised that he did not seem to understand what was said to him and his language was very immature. They felt that his behaviour was linked to frustration. An assessment by a speech and language therapist suggested that Jonathan's language was in fact quite disordered and that he was having genuine difficulties in making sense of what was said to him or in ordering his own words when speaking to others. He is about to start an intensive programme working with a support assistant in the group, following a specialist approach advised by the therapist.

▲ ● ■ Holly

Holly is four and speaks fluently at home. However, she is virtually silent in the setting and speaks only occasionally to one other child when in the home corner. She seems otherwise quite settled and happy in the group though becomes sullen if pressed to speak. Her key person has begun to get to know Holly much more closely, visiting her at home and trying to work out just where Holly will speak and where she will not. It seems that she is very anxious about hearing her own voice in certain situations. As far as the setting can tell, her language development at home seems normal.

▲ ● ■ All different

Here we have three children, each with a different set of difficulties and needs. All are described as having speech and language difficulties, though each will require a very different approach. In this chapter, we will find out what some of the barriers to their learning might be.

▲ ● ■ Speech and language development

Speech and language development is an intriguing process. Most children appear to acquire language and speech in a remarkably uniform way and seem to be almost 'pre-programmed' to acquire speech sounds, grammar and meaning and to want to communicate socially. Their whole brain structure seems to be geared towards acquiring language and their language system seems geared towards helping them find out as much about their world as possible. As they find out more and their language skills develop, they become able to 'internalise' their language so that thinking, reasoning and predicting inside their heads becomes possible and so that they can use their internal language and thinking to direct their actions. Yet, for some children, this does not happen spontaneously.

Speech and language difficulties occur for many different reasons. There might be a lack of opportunity for development because of deprivation or emotional causes; there might be a hearing loss or physical disability; a general difficulty in learning and development; or difficulties even in the absence of these causes. This last group of children is sometimes described as having a 'specific developmental disorder of speech and language', 'language impairment' or a 'specific language disorder'. Some children also have difficulties in communicating because English is not their first language; this book is not about these children, though some of the activity ideas may be helpful.

▲ ● ■ Communication and language strands

The *Communicating Matters* materials and training were produced as part of SureStart and the Primary National Strategy and launched in September 2005. They give us a new way of viewing language and communication development within the EYFS and define certain 'strands' of communication and language to help us to tune into children's language and therefore encourage it. Many LEAs and SureStart services are now providing this training or at least embedding the principles within the support services that they provide to settings. The four strands of communication and language are:

- Knowing and using sounds and signs
- Knowing and using words
- Structuring language
- Making language work.

We can look at each of these in turn and see how children typically develop in each strand. This helps us to identify children who might be following a different pathway to language and communication and to plan additional different approaches to support them.

▲ ● ■ Knowing and using sounds and signs

In the earliest stages of development, babies begin to make and develop a range of sounds that gradually become more speech-like as they grow older. Here are the typical ages and stages:

- 0–4 months: babies produce different cries, their different cries begin to develop as signals to their carers and they begin to make sounds in response to faces, music or other sounds around them.
- 4–6 months: babies develop a wider range of vocalisations and responses.
- 6–10 months: babies start 'babbling' (repeating strings of sound) and begin to respond to some words (such as 'Look at Mum') with sounds and actions of their own.

- 8 months+: babies begin to form some speech sounds (such as da-da-da and bi-bi-bi and realise that speech is used to communicate with.
- 9–12 months: a baby's babbling sounds become more speech-like and they are increasingly responsive when spoken to.
- 10–13 months: babies are usually able to use sounds, pointing, gaze and reaching out to communicate and share interests.
- 10–24 months: most children begin to say some recognisable words.
- 2 years+: the children's speech sounds get clearer although there are still some immaturities between certain sounds such as r/l or s/sh.

▲ ● ■ When there are difficulties

Some children have speech and language difficulties associated with not speaking clearly. Dillan, whom we met at the beginning of the chapter, has these difficulties. This is a form of 'expressive' language difficulty as it affects the way the child's speech and language are expressed (as opposed to 'receptive' difficulties which are linked to poor understanding). A child with expressive difficulties may have failed to develop certain speech sounds or perhaps cannot sequence or coordinate strings of sounds properly. Perhaps the child's language can only be understood by those who know the child really well and where there is a shared context so that the listener knows what the child is talking about. These children are sometimes described as having 'dyspraxic', 'dysarthric' or 'articulation' difficulties, depending on the cause.

Speech and language therapy can help these children to learn and practise new sounds and it is helpful if teachers can link closely with any ongoing therapy so that activities can be planned around the therapy goals. For example, some children benefit from activities that help them to hear the rhythm of syllables and language. Number rhymes and action rhymes are most beneficial. The use of symbols, pictures or real objects can be used when the child is asked to make a choice or to plan their learning and play activities. Hearing back the correct enunciation of a word (without being asked to repeat it) can provide the child with the correct model of the word and also help the listener to clarify what the child was trying to say. Patient listening and interpretation is called for, with plenty of opportunities for the child to succeed in areas of learning that do not involve language. If their speech is very unclear, the speech and language therapist might recommend that these children be taught to use a simple language programme with signing. This is not used to replace their speech but to help other people to understand the words they are trying to communicate so that they can respond appropriately.

▲ ● ■ Knowing and using words

As well as building up and using a wide repertoire of speech sounds and signs, children must learn to string these together to form words. How do children typically develop in learning and using new words?

• Up to 12 months: babies respond to some familiar words such as 'dada' or 'dog'.

• 9–12 months: babies will recognise key words and it is about now that their first words are spoken.

• 13 months: most children have an average of about 10 words.

• 14–17 months: the average increases to around 50 words, but this varies enormously.

• 18 months: most children have acquired around 100 words.

• 12–24 months: children's use of pointing and gesture develops separately. They use some 'jargon' – their own words that they have developed and which they use with consistency (such as 'ging gang' for 'granny'). Word combinations (such as 'Mama car') start when they have reached 50–100 words.

• 24–36 months: the range of words is so wide that anything between 40 to 600 words is all normal.

• 30–36 months: children have an average of 150 words and are learning new vocabulary at a rate of 3 to 10 new words a day. They will use gesture alongside words.

• 3–6 years: there is a rapid increase in vocabulary. Politeness begins to develop ('Can I …?') as well as concept words and abstract vocabulary. Children begin to handle more complex language such as if/because phrases and question words.

▲ ● ■ When there are difficulties

Children with expressive language difficulties might use very short phrases, or have difficulties in remembering the names of things. They might use general descriptions such as 'thing' rather than the label. Their speech might sound immature even though they have developed age-appropriate skills in other areas. They tend to lose fluency when they are excited or stressed, and talk best in a relaxed situation. Some children stutter and this becomes worse if they feel pressured or if attention is drawn to it. Again, your patience and sensitivity is called for and you should never jump in to complete their sentences for them. These children need your encouragement to slow down and regulate their speech in a relaxed and unhurried atmosphere.

▲ ● ■ Structuring language

Once children have developed a range of speech sounds, formed these into words and built up a vocabulary of words that they can use, they have to learn how to structure their words into sentences and phrases in order to communicate clearly with others. Here are the typical stages they go through:

• 12 months+: children tend to use one word to represent many things (such as 'dog' being used to represent all animals) – these are known as 'holophrases'.
• 18–24 months: children seem to be looking for word patterns and will play with new combinations that they have found ('my car'; 'my ball'). Multi-word combinations begin to be formed such as 'Daddy bike' and they begin to respond to questions and directions.
• 24–36 months: children's language becomes more grammatical with the appearance of negatives (no/not) and questions.
• 3 years+: children can now use lots of connecting words and are able to respond to more complex language from others.
• 3–6 years: there is a growing sophistication as children's language is used for many different functions and purposes.

▲ ● ■ When there are difficulties

For some children, language remains shortened like a telegram because they do not naturally acquire the grammar and 'order' that language usually follows. Sometimes this is because their language development is delayed, but nevertheless progressing along normal lines. Perhaps these children are delayed in other areas of their development as well and the language delay is just one part of this immaturity. Activities that help the child progress step by small step will be the most helpful, making sure that the child has a chance to succeed and develop confidence at each stage.

For other children, there is a specific language 'disorder'. Jonathan, whom we met at the beginning of the chapter, has a specific difficulty. For children such as Jonathan, their understanding of language (and especially abstract language such as 'more', 'full' and other concept words) is usually affected, as well as their use of language. A speech and language therapist usually will be involved and will be able to advise you on approaches. Sometimes these children will be offered intensive speech, language and communication programmes at a speech and language unit and then return to their local school for ongoing support once they have overcome some of their difficulties.

Children with comprehension or 'receptive language difficulties' can be difficult to detect. You might think that they understand everything you say, yet, on close examination, you find that they are responding to a host of other clues rather than to the words alone. Test this out by offering no clues: 'Fetch your coat' might well gain a response at the end of the session when everyone is getting ready to go home, but would it gain the same response if you said it in the middle of the session?

▲ ● ■ Making language work

As well as developing sounds, words and sentences, children must learn how to make their language work for others so that they can communicate effectively with it. They must learn how to use language socially, how to hold a conversation, how to signal that they want to say something, how to use language for thinking and problem solving and how to enjoy and share language together. Here are the typical ages and stages.

• Babies: they begin to understand turn-taking and it is possible to hold 'baby conversations' with them, echoing their words back to them as they wait for your response. They will usually turn their eyes or heads to locate the speaker.
• 18 months: children begin to respond to very simple requests such as 'where are your shoes?'
• 24 months+: children begin to assess what the other person knows and share their interests with them.
• 24–36 months: children can usually retell simple events.
• 36 months+: by now most children can initiate and maintain a conversation using discourse markers such as 'well…' or 'um…'.
• 4 years+: children can use many resources and devices in their language (for example, 'Once upon a time…'). They can work out what information is needed from a questioner, assess listeners' perspectives, answer questions and 'think out loud'.
• 5 years+: children can now 'repair' conversations by clarifying what has been said and rewording phrases. They can use language very imaginatively in their play.

▲ ● ■ When there are difficulties

Quite often, children who have specific language difficulties also have difficulties in understanding social situations, in seeing the other point of view, in using their imaginations and in handling conversations. These are sometimes describes as 'pragmatic difficulties'. Many of the activities in this book aim to improve children's pragmatic skills and there are more ideas in the book *Autistic Spectrum Disorders* (Scholastic), in this series.

▲ ● ■ When speech and language do not develop easily

Whereas all children in EYFS are still mastering their use and understanding of language, you might feel that some have difficulties that go beyond what you might normally expect from their age and stage, even though they have had the opportunity to learn. You may be right to be concerned and to plan additional and different approaches when, for example, a child:

• cannot speak clearly and can only be understood by those who know her really well

• has a very limited vocabulary and either fails to use or to understand words that most children his age have learned

• can only speak in very short phrases or 'like a telegram' so that her speech is at an earlier developmental level than for most other children

• can only understand very simple language and instructions or needs you always to show him what to do as well as tell him

• cannot grasp the meaning of abstract language such as 'heavy', 'full' or 'same'

• cannot use language imaginatively or in conversations so that her language is used in a very concrete and inflexible way

• cannot grasp how to ask or answer questions, perhaps because he has not understood the question word itself (what/where/why/who/which/when)

• has not grasped the social dynamics of speaking with someone else, failing to judge the turn-taking property of language, how to regulate her voice, how close to stand and how the listener might be thinking

• has not yet learned how to regulate his attention so that he can listen, hold on to the information spoken to him and then respond

• cannot speak fluently and stammers or avoids speaking altogether

• is very specific about where, when and to whom she will speak. This is sometimes known as 'selective mutism'. Holly, whom we met at the beginning of the chapter, has these difficulties.

▲ ● ■ How many children are affected?

Because of the differences between professionals in how they define the population of children with specific speech and language difficulties, it is difficult to be precise about prevalence. About 3 to 15 per cent of children in the UK experience some form of difficulty in acquiring language, though 40 per cent resolve these problems by the middle of their first year in school. It seems that some children overcome an initial delay fairly early on, but others go on to experience later literacy and language difficulties if their early problems do not resolve. In one study, 60 per cent of children who had language difficulties during their pre-school years continued to exhibit language problems at the age of ten and even beyond. The prognosis was poorest for those who had general learning difficulties as well. Your on-going assessment of how each child in your class learns and progresses will help you to tease out those children who have general delay as well as speech and language delay and will enable you to target your support for those most at risk.

▲ ● ■ Potential barriers

What are the barriers that these children face and what does this mean for your practice?

• Some children might find it hard to interact and communicate in a large group – they might interact with you in quieter situations or benefit from being in a smaller group for some of the time.

• You might not realise at first just how delayed a child's speech or understanding might be. This means that they will not be responding to the language in the setting at an appropriate level and you may not be meeting their needs within the EYFS. Time and careful assessment are needed to tune in to a child's level of speech and language development.

• The child might find it hard to take in, process and respond to language at a normal speed and you will find yourself having to pace yourself to match the child's speed of processing.

• Some children with language difficulties are not stretched as far as they might be because there is always someone there to interpret or 'speak for them'. You will find it best to take a moment or two to observe how the child is interacting and playing before you make any assumptions about what they can and cannot do. Never underestimate how much children can help each other – they may be managing fine without you!

• Some children cannot cope with the amount of language or its complexity in a busy setting. That is not to say that they should not be there. You will find yourself keeping your language simple, emphasising key words and showing children what to do as well as telling them.

• Some children struggle to make themselves understood but would become frustrated (or give up trying) if you were to constantly correct them. You will need to model correct pronunciation and format and rephrase the correct version after they have spoken so that they hear how to say things correctly but do not feel nagged.

• Some children for whom English is not their first or only language go through a silent patch for a while and speak very little in the setting. Do not worry – continue to involve them fully and to model language for them as this is a very normal phase.

• Some children will not respond to group instructions as if they do not realise that they are included in the instructions or because they have poor comprehension or listening skills. Address the child individually, having engaged their attention first. Check for understanding by testing this out one-to-one. Arrange for hearing to be checked if you are at all concerned.

• Some children cannot grasp the meaning of abstract vocabulary that cannot actually be pointed at or touched (for example, descriptive words or adverbs). Link action to abstract words where possible (for example, design activities to teach 'quietly' or 'gently').

• Some children might need non-verbal methods of communicating side by side with language development. Consider using signing as an aid to language development, after liaising with parents and a speech and language therapist. Most signing systems work to encourage spoken language and aid understanding rather than to replace it in any way.

In the next chapter, we will explore in more detail how you can help to remove the barriers that children with speech and language difficulties might face in your setting.

Removing the Barriers

Each child with speech and language difficulties is an individual and you will need to tune into their particular needs in order to remove as many barriers to their early learning as possible.

▲ ● ■ Creating the Right Environment for Language Development

What can you do in general terms to make your setting the right place to foster children's speech and language development?

• Encourage confidence in all the children. Confident children are more likely to talk and find communication less threatening. Everything that you do to encourage close relationships between staff and children, establish secure routines and take children's own choices into account will also help the children's language development flow more smoothly.

• Be aware of noise levels in your rooms. High noise levels can get in the way of successful communication. You need to plan activities so that they do not interfere with each other and aim to reduce the overall noise levels by using absorbent soft surfaces where possible.

• Create a noise-free area for quiet work and talking if you can.

• Try to become more aware of your own listening and talking skills. Do you take the time to listen carefully to each child? Do you provide a good model of language for the children to follow? Have you developed a communication style that promotes interaction, encourages, enables and stimulates children to talk with you? Try to listen to what the child is telling you, rather than how the child is saying it.

• Look for ways of making language and communication meaningful and fun. Make sure that the child enjoys talking, use constant praise and reassurance and ignore mistakes by modelling the correct version instead.

▲ ● ■ Top Tips for Overcoming Barriers

Even if you have created the best environment for language development, there will still be children who find it hard to make progress. Here are some key strategies and approaches borrowed from what we know about speech and language difficulties and the techniques on offer. If there is a speech and language therapist involved, always liaise first so that you know which are the best approaches for the child's particular set of difficulties.

Being patient

You may need to wait longer than usual, or to patiently repeat what has been said before a child responds to what you have asked for. Give a child with a language processing difficulty time to respond or to imitate before you come in with a repetition or the answer. Sometimes a 'Makaton' language programme involving signing is used in order to make instructions and requests clearer (see page 8).

Some children opt to speak in one situation and not another – this is sometimes called selective mutism. Be patient and never try to force the child to speak. Visit the child at home if you can in order to hear them talk there. Offer non-verbal ways of responding in your group such as a nod or a hand up at register. Once you have a

nod/shake, move on to expecting the child to indicate choices. Above all, allow these children to develop speaking in their own time – if they feel anxious about hearing their own voices, then other people's anxiety will only make things worse.

Choices

Offer choices or alternatives when asking questions of a child with a severe expressive language difficulty (such as 'Do you want to finish your story or work on your model?'). Illustrations and concrete props can help the development of vocabulary. Help parents and carers to offer their child choices (and to develop language, confidence and relationships at the same time) using the 'Supportive Play' format. See page 87 for a photocopiable sheet to take home.

Cue children's listening

Explain to the children what is involved in good listening (staying still, looking at the speaker and thinking about what has been said). Focus the children's attention onto what is being said by slowing down your pace, repeating important points and reinforcing important information by providing visual prompts (for example, pointing to a book when you ask a child to fetch a book) or giving situational clues (for example, pointing outside when you ask the child to fetch their coat).

Ditch the dummy

There are many children whose language development has become delayed simply through lack of opportunity to speak. Dummies can become a real habit within families and stubbornly difficult to get rid of (see the Play plan on page 31 for some general ideas). For children who are now old enough to manage without, try a joint parent-setting initiative to become a dummy-free environment! One group created a 'magic dummy tree' and involved a persona doll called Molly to hang her dummy on the tree only to find it had transformed into a little teddy bear the next day. Within a week, each and every child brought in a dummy for the tree and delighted in its 'magic'. When you work in a group like this, the confrontation is removed and everyone supports each other.

Double meanings

Children with a language disorder often find it hard to understand double meaning, sarcasm, metaphor or irony. They may interpret it too literally and become confused. Avoid ambiguous requests such as 'Would you like to sit down now?' Replace this with 'Ashley – sit down please'. Make sure that your instructions are concrete, direct and explicit and support these with picture prompts if necessary. Give examples of any double meanings and give an explanation for humour and metaphor if you have to.

Engaging attention

Children with language and communication difficulties often have poor looking and listening skills. Say their name clearly, get down to their level, try to encourage eye contact albeit briefly (to signal your intent to communicate) and then speak. When you are issuing instructions to the whole group, address the child with difficulties by name first to engage attention. Give very clear and simple messages, showing the child as well as telling her what to do.

Eye contact

Encourage eye contact by using the child's name, a gentle touch on his shoulder and by speaking at his level, face to face. Praise him for looking at you when you speak to him and also encourage him to look at you when he is speaking to you. Help the child to stay on subject if he tends to wander off it. Gently point out that you need to listen to the other children too, using a gentle hand-hold perhaps, to show that you are still 'there' for him while he waits his turn to speak. From time to time, alter your level so that you can play face to face with a child and use your eye contact to share the fun.

Expand children's thinking

If you are playing together with a toy or activity, expand the child's thinking and language by offering further information to help the child learn more. For example (depending on the child's language level) if playing with a train, you can:

- label: 'that's a train'
- describe: 'that train has stopped'
- explain: 'your mum goes on a train to work'
- pretend: 'let's pretend these chairs are a train'
- talk about feelings: 'you like trains, don't you!'
- talk about the future: 'I'll bring in a photo of a steam train tomorrow'
- project: 'when you're grown up perhaps you'll go on a train every day'.

Extend imagination

Look for opportunities to help the child think and play imaginatively and to develop symbolic skills. This is especially helpful if the child can learn to play imaginatively with another child, providing opportunities for developing their own imaginative ideas and language. Encourage imaginative thinking and pretend play by basing this on 'real life' experiences at first. You might act out going to a party together or visiting the supermarket. Small-world play and role play can also be helpful and will mean that other children enjoy the learning situation as well.

Facilitate joining in

Support a child with speech and language difficulties to join in with other children by staying close and making suggestions. You may need to interpret what the child is saying to their peers in order to sustain the interaction. Look for ways of making the social learning more enjoyable for everyone; some activities can only be carried out if there is more then one child, and some are simply more fun!

Give it time

Some children stammer or stutter when they are speaking and this becomes worse when they are rushed, pressured or feeling self-conscious. Listen patiently to what

the child is saying and try very hard not to interrupt or complete their thoughts for them. Keep looking at the child as you listen, and reply slowly and unhurriedly after a second or two's pause; this slows the whole exchange to a more relaxed tempo. Never hurry the child's speech or keep the child from speaking if he or she is keen to tell you all something. If the child has a hand up at talking time, let them answer fairly soon to prevent anxiety building up. Many children with speech and language difficulties benefit from having the pace of the exchange slowed down, so that they have time to coordinate their listening, thinking and speaking.

Imitation

For children at an earlier stage of language and communication, spend time copying what they do, how they play and what vocalisations they make. In time, they might notice what you are doing and start to imitate you in turn. When you imitate a child's sounds and actions, the child knows that you are interested and will start to look at and listen to you more carefully.

Interpretation

The child might not know the words for what is happening, but you do, and you can help by saying the things that you know the child would say if only they could. At the same time, if you genuinely do not know what a child is trying to say, you need to be honest and encourage the child to find ways of making it clearer. For younger children who have difficulty in making their needs known, appoint a key person to get to know that child well and to find out about the way they communicate and make their needs known. This key person will then be able to interpret the child's actions and act on them consistently, thereby ensuring that any signalling of need becomes meaningful and intentional. This key person can also put together a 'communication book' (with photographs and descriptions) showing all staff the signs, expressions, words or behaviours that a child uses in order to communicate their feelings and needs.

Keep it concrete

It is easier to understand what the child is trying to tell you if you are talking about things you have done or shared together. Use props and photographs from home to trigger talk about the child's 'news'. Use illustrations and real objects to introduce topics. Build in subjects that really interest the child. Try to relate talk to everyday objects, names and activities in the 'here and now'. Introduce words for objects, actions, smells, colours and textures as you try new learning activities.

Label everything

Look for opportunities to say the names of everyday objects whenever you can. For example, instead of asking 'Do you want this or that?' say 'Do you want the cloak or the scarf?', holding each up in turn. Instead of asking constant questions ('What colour is this?'; 'What's this called?') observe what the child is interested in and describe it yourself – 'You've chosen the red engine today'.

Non-verbal modelling

Children can be shown (as well as told) what to do in any structured learning situation. Even during open-ended play they will benefit from an adult playing alongside from time to time. The adult will be modelling new and flexible ways of playing and communicating or providing a commentary to help them link language with action. Children with speech and language difficulties sometimes also have difficulties with fine motor coordination and you may need to show the child how to use a pencil or paintbrush, how to enjoy writing and artwork, and even how to become more personally independent.

Parent power

You will find some helpful handouts for parents at the end of the book. The effect that you have on a child's language development in the setting will more than double if you can also work in partnership with parents and carers. Early intervention goes a long way to preventing long-term speech and language difficulties. Many LEAs are developing programmes and resources to use in partnership with parents. One LEA uses themed bags for parents to take home, containing a book to share, a game or toy, activities to promote language development and simple instruction sheets for parents and carers. The bags can be sent home with children who have been identified as having some delay in language development. They aim to support these children at home as well as in the setting, providing fun activities and reinforcing learning. They are designed to raise parents' awareness of language

delay and how to overcome it. This is simple to set up and organise – why not liaise with your local speech and language therapy service or SureStart to try such a scheme in your setting?

Peer support

Children whose speech and language development is progressing normally are excellent models for children who have difficulties. Draw attention to other children's questions and comments and support the child with difficulties in responding, learning cooperatively or initiating ideas themselves. Start in a small group of two children for certain activities and gradually extend the size of the group. Some of the activities in this book suggest small groups, but you may find that you can try larger groups once progress has been made.

Play power

You will probably find that the child uses language most fluently during play and free activity times. Allow the child to develop language and conversation skills both independently and also when supported by you. Look for occasions when you can use language together in a non-direct way, perhaps by talking easily and informally while the child is involved in a creative activity or in the home corner.

Reassurance

Provide a higher level of reassurance. Children with language difficulties are more likely to lack confidence and feel insecure in a social setting. They may even find other children unpredictable or frightening because they have not learned the simple rules of social behaviour or lack words to express themselves. They will feel more confident if a friend or familiar adult is close by. Working or playing with a partner can be really helpful.

Running commentary

From time to time, work alongside the child with speech and language difficulties and provide a simple spoken commentary of what he or she is doing. This provides opportunities for the child to link actions with words and can also help other children to interpret what the child is doing and saying. Keep your language simple and at the child's level of understanding, emphasising key words appropriately. It may be tempting to bombard children with questions but this is particularly difficult for many children with language difficulties as they do not understand the meaning of question words such as 'what', 'why' or 'which'.

Starting points

Get to know the child well in order to have a clear starting point for your support. Talk with parents or carers and find out about how much the child understands and how well they can express themselves. How do they make their needs known? Ask parents to record some language at home (where the child is most relaxed) so that you can have a 'feel' of the stage they have reached even if the child says very little in school. Get in touch with any speech and language therapist involved to share assessments and targets.

Simplify requests

Keep your requests short and simple by breaking them down into shorter chunks or rephrasing them. Try to remain encouraging. For example, if you say 'Go and fetch The Three Bears' and the child returns with any book, say 'Thank you – you've brought a book – now can you remember which book?' If a child fails to respond to a question like 'Where's the shop assistant?', try a simpler version: 'Show me the man who works in the shop'. Alternatively, offer a choice – 'Does this man work in the shop or on the farm?'

Starting early

It is never too soon to start encouraging language development, especially for the parents and carers you work with. There is a parent handout on communicating during the first year of life on the photocopiable page 90. Why not share this with carers and see whether you work preventatively? In each activity section there is at least one play plan for babies for those of you that work with children at risk of language delay, for example in Sure Start services.

Support planning and persistence

Take time to support children in planning what they are going to do next. For example, if you are about to make a poster together, talk about what it will show and who it will be for. Focus on how you will make it. Then focus on how you will display it. Help them to see this through and evaluate how it has gone and what they think about it.

Teach reciprocity

For a child who lacks the skills of verbal and social interaction, look for opportunities to encourage the development of turn-taking. This important skill leads on to language and conversation later. Simple 'my turn, your turn' activities and board games help this skill to develop. Drama and role play are excellent ways to develop this and you can also build in many opportunities during circle-time.

Teach sequencing

When you are sharing story books together, spend time discussing the story and predicting what might happen next. Encourage children to retell the story in their own way, gradually building up to longer sequences. Perhaps at first, for example, a child might predict what is beneath the flap in a familiar 'lift-the-flap' book. In time, they might tell you a whole section of the story and remember what happens at the end of the story as well. Digital photography can be a useful way of helping children to develop planning and sequencing skills and can be used as a comic strip in order to provide information to the child.

Teach social skills

Identify which behaviour you need to change and decide what new behaviour needs to be taught in its place. Children might need to learn how to make their voices loud or soft when talking and not to shout or whisper all the time. They may need to learn to look at you when speaking and how close to stand. They may need to be shown how to be 'gentle', how to greet other children without being too shy or too overwhelming, how to pass a pencil to another child rather than throwing it, or how to ask for something rather than grabbing it. Teach the children how to gain attention appropriately with an 'excuse me' rather than a direct interruption.

Time to talk

Encourage conversations by spending quiet moments together and encouraging simple turn-taking in what you say; some children find it hard to learn the 'flow' of speaking first, then listening. Use small group work to encourage simple conversations with other children and try to relate the conversations to something concrete that everyone knows about at first. Encourage the child with disordered language to describe things in an organised way by keeping your commentary well organised: Who was involved? Where are they? What are they doing? What happened next?

Tune in to language levels

The best help that you can give the child will be your own language, but delivered at just the right level of complexity for the child to understand it and respond to it. Use simple key-words that you know the child understands. Rephrase instructions that have been given to the whole group, keeping them concrete and showing the child what to do as well, so that the child is using a multi-sensory approach.

Verbal modelling

It is helpful for a child with expressive language difficulties to hear correct models of what they are trying to say. For example, if the child tells you that 'The quinpin catched the fish', repeat back 'Yes, the penguin caught the fish!'– emphasising the word that was mispronounced or incorrectly said. Do not constantly correct the child and never be tempted to use the child's version of a word, however cute it sounds.

Verbal prompts

When the child is trying to remember a word, you can help by suggesting other clues ('What did it look like?'; 'What was it for?') to help the child develop descriptions. Sometimes just providing the initial sound ('It's a c…') can be enough to help them retrieve the word they are searching for.

Visual timetables

You can help a child with language and communication difficulties by showing pictures or symbols about what is going to happen next. Make a series of cards with Velcro backs that can be arranged in line on a felt board or use a whiteboard to talk about and draw the session's timetable at its beginning. You can also use this board to offer choices to a child who has little expressive language.

While reading through these strategies, you might have found yourself picturing certain children with speech and language difficulties whom you work with. 'Mix and match' the ideas until you find an approach that is tailor-made for the child concerned.

Language for Communication

CLL

Many children who have speech and language difficulties will need additional support in order to help them to communicate clearly, effectively and socially.

▲ ● ■ Links to Area of Learning

We saw in the first chapter how babies and young children learn how to communicate in a variety of ways as they begin to create their own personal sounds and words before going on to form real words, which they can later string together. Over the first few years, these words are used to convey simple and then more complex messages. Most language emerges around matters that are personally important, interesting and meaningful for the child and this is where your planning becomes so important – in selecting activities and providing opportunities for children to be at their most verbal. Children who have speech and language difficulties might find it hard to make their language understood by others and this can be both frustrating and off-putting for them. Your role becomes one of making sure that confidence is not lost at this stage, to model correct speech, to interpret the child to others and to help the child use other methods such as gesture and sign to make their meaning clearer. Look for other methods of responding for a child who cannot discuss and explain. For example, stories can be retold using comic strip cartoons as well as with words or acted out using movements and gestures. Be alert to vocabulary that might be missing so that you can plan opportunities for introducing and reinforcing new words.

▲ ● ■ How to use the play plans

You will find an assessment sheet for working out which skills and competencies the child has already acquired on the next two pages. Look out for behaviours that are sometimes, but not yet always, demonstrated and work on these as a starting point. On the assessment sheets on pages 26 and 27 you will notice that six skills are marked with an asterisk. On pages 29 to 34 you will find a play plan for each of the six skills marked. If you need to focus on a skill not covered by a play plan, then you will find a blank photocopiable sheet on page 85; the activities and strategies in this book should help you to draw up your own. Each play plan contains eight interventions that you could try. Some play plans are designed to be followed in a specific order and are numbered as such. Other play plans may be dipped into to suit individual circumstances – these are marked with a DIP IN icon. There are also two blank spaces to add your own personalised interventions onto each play plan. If you wish to be selective, use a highlighter to flag up those parts of the play plan that you would like colleagues to concentrate on. If you wish to use the play plan for monitoring, use a dating and initialling system to record who did what and when. This can link into your progress monitoring and summary sheets on page 86 and 88 and be shared with parents and carers using the sheet on page 87. The same simple format is followed in all of the activity chapters.

Assessment sheet: Language for Communication

Name:................................. Key person:...................

Communication, Language and Literacy

Language for Communication and Thinking: Language for Communication

enter date observed

Development matters	What I do now	Never	Sometimes	Always
Making sounds	Make a range of speech-like sounds			
	Babble (repeat sounds over and over)*			
First words	Have a vocabulary of a few single words			
	Use these words at appropriate times			
	Look at an object when you use its word			
	Respond to 'give me' a named familiar object			
	Use 50 single words, mostly clear			
	Use 100 clear words			
Early Communication	Turn my body or head away to indicate 'no'			
	Look at the speaker			
	Wait for the speaker to reply before vocalising again			
	Use a different tone of voice to suit what is being said*			
	Hold a short two-way conversation			
	Stringing words together			
	Use two words together			
	Respond to two word phrases, such as 'more drink'			
	Use short phrases			
	Speak in short sentences			
	Use plurals, sometimes incorrectly still			
	Use negatives (such as no/not)			
Initiating communication	Use a single word to request things			
	Willing to come into the group without a dummy*			
	Use names to engage other people's attention			
	Use communication to initiate play			

	Volunteer information in a small group
	Listen in to interesting discussion from others
	Chatter freely in certain situations
Stories and rhymes	Enjoy action rhymes
	Join in some actions
	Anticipate what comes next*
	Join in repeated refrains
	Listen to stories with interest
	Retell a story using actions or words
Questioning	Answer questions using cloze procedure (Jo would like to play with the …?')
	Ask and answer simple 'what? questions
	Ask and answer simple 'who?' questions
	Ask and answer simple 'where?' questions*
	Ask and answer simple 'why?' questions
	Ask and answer simple 'when?' questions
Possession	Use my own name to indicate possession (for example, 'Ahmed's!')
	Use other children's names to indicate possession
	Use me/mine
	Use you/yours
	Use his/her, him/her
Flexible language	Use language in free play
	Confident to chat to familiar others
	Use gestures to clarify what is being said*
	Willing to speak to a new staff member
	Use language to retell an event
	Use language to be polite (such as please/ thank you)

Early Learning Goals:

Interact with others, negotiating plans and activities and taking turns in conversation.
Extend their vocabulary, exploring the meanings and sounds of new words.
Speak clearly and audibly with confidence and control and show awareness of the listener, for example, by their use of conventions such as greetings, 'please' and 'thank you'.

▲ ● ■ Look, listen and note

It is helpful for all the children if you look for opportunities to observe their play and early learning and note down how they are progressing. For children who have speech and language difficulties, here are some things to look out for in particular. You might find the observation sheet on page 89 helpful to copy and use for all kinds of observations.

• Observe when and how a baby vocalises. Do the vocalisations increase when there is someone or something interesting to watch? What sounds can the baby make and can you tell what any cries or noises actually mean yet (such as 'I need my nappy changing' or 'Feed me!')?

• Observe the gestures that the child is making. Does the child try hard to make his or her needs known, either by repeating what was said or using gestures to make it clearer?

• Does the child pay attention to words? Do you notice the child responding to key words, following simple directions, or turning to look at others when their name is called?

• Are you satisfied that the child can hear properly? Some children's hearing varies from day to day, depending on colds and so on. Test this out in different situations – responding to whispers in a quiet room, turning to you across a room when you speak their name or turning to a rustling crisp packet or rumbling drum. Speak with parents and/or a health visitor if you are concerned.

• Watch the child at story time. Does the child appear to be following the story line? What is your evidence for thinking this? Can the child 'retell' the story, either through gestures, sequencing pictures (with your support) or using language?

▲ ● ■ Effective practice

• Try to arrange your room so that there are quiet distraction-free areas for small group activities as well as larger, noisier spaces. Use carpets, cushions and curtains to absorb sound.

• Look for ways of linking words with pictures or actions so that the child makes links between new words and their meanings.

• Plan for a regular circle time with sharing games, talking time and action rhymes.

• Always get down to the child's level, establish eye contact and use a name and a light touch before you say anything important.

• Allow time to hold conversations with the child, slowing your pace down to suit their ability and level of understanding.

• Make contact with any speech and language therapist involved so that you can share approaches and targets or build their advice into any individual education plan for the child.

• Use a home-setting diary so that you can keep in touch with interesting events in the child's life at home and talk about these together in the setting.

Dip in

Play plan: Beautiful babbling!

Name: ....   **Key person:** ....

Area of Learning: CLL   **Focus: Language for communication**   **Individual target: Babble (repeat sounds over and over)**

Play silly face games as you make noises – blowing raspberries or making blubbery noises with your lips and fingers. Share the fun as ☺ makes sounds back to you.

Hold ☺ up to a large mirror and encourage vocalisations.

Play 'peep-bo', staying silent when your face is covered, but making lots of sounds when you reappear. See if ☺ does the same when you use a light scarf to cover ☺'s face.

Note the times when ☺ is more likely to vocalise and set up this activity in a quiet area with a small group so that ☺ can hear their own voice.

Respond with delight if ☺ makes a long string of sounds and stop what you are doing to give ☺ plenty of attention and to echo it back.

Try singing softly to ☺ and then pause for ☺ to make sing-song noises back to you.

Hold ☺ on your knee, facing you. Smile and share cuddles as you echo back each sound that ☺ makes. Pause expectantly to encourage ☺ to make the next sound.

Make soft sounds together to favourite soft toys and encourage ☺ to 'talk' to them as you give them a cuddle.

Dip in

Play plan: Setting the tone

Name: .... **Key person:** ....

Area of Learning: CLL   Focus: Language for communication   **Individual target: Use a different tone of voice to suit what is being said**

Encourage ☺ to retell a favourite story to a younger child in the book corner in whatever way ☺ can, using the different tone of voices involved.

Use role play to practise speaking with expression and using tone of voice imaginatively.

Give the characters in your small-world play different characters, voices and ways of speaking.

Try the 'Voices' rhyme. You say, 'Have you got your LOUD voices?' and the children reply (loudly), 'YES WE HAVE!' Introduce quiet/happy/ sad/grumpy/whiny and so on.

Use puppet play so that ☺ can practise speaking in different voices for different characters.

If ☺ begins to shout louder and louder while speaking with you, continue to reply in a quiet voice rather than become louder yourself.

Teach 'loud voice' and 'quiet voice' and remind ☺ to use a quiet voice when speaking to you or a loud voice when calling everyone in from outside.

Exaggerate tones of voice when you tell stories and ask the children how they think your character is feeling.

Dip in

Play plan: Deposit the dummy

Name: ....

Key person: ....

Area of Learning: CLL   Focus: Language for communication

Individual target: Willing to come into the group without a dummy

Give colourful certificates or stickers: 'I don't need my dummy in the group any more!'

Enlist the parents/carers support— they are probably as keen as you to see the end of the dummy if their child is now old enough. Suggest saving it for rest and bedtimes now.

If ☺ is fretting for the dummy, try offering ☺ a drink instead.

Try making a 'magic dummy tree' together. Encourage the children to hang their dummies on and make sure they turn magically into something special the next day!

If ☺ asks you for something whilst wearing the dummy, explain that you cannot hear. Ask for a repeat without the dummy.

Wear a giant dummy for the session yourself and mumble through it to the children. See what they say!

Have a special dummy pot for each child and make depositing it there part of the regular routine. Distract immediately with something new and fun to play with instead.

At circle time, try using a puppet that has a large dummy. Wait for the children themselves to suggest that the puppet should take the dummy out as they can't hear the puppet!

Dip in

Play plan: And next...

Name: .... Key person: ....

Area of Learning: CLL   Focus: Language for communication   Individual target: Anticipate what comes next

Use photographs of ☺ busy at an activity. Show them in sequence and see if ☺ can guess what happened next.

Tell a favourite story over and over on different days. After a while, pause to let ☺ anticipate the next page, using voice, gesture or facial expression.

Use puppet or role play to set up scenarios. Encourage ☺'s puppet to respond by anticipating what comes next (for example, getting the bed ready because your puppet is tired).

Use familiar action rhymes and again pause for ☺ to come in with the next action or word.

Encourage ☺ to think ahead about becoming independent. Instead of 'Put your coat on, we're going outside', say 'We're going outside. What do you need?'

Use digital photography to create picture timetables of your regular routine and use these to help ☺ anticipate what comes next or to make choices.

Once ☺ is familiar with your regular routine, encourage ☺ to tell you what happens next. Give ☺ little jobs to help the other children so that ☺ is involved fully in the routine.

Introduce novel situations to ☺ and encourage ☺ to anticipate what might happen (for example, 'There's no more paper to paint on. What shall we do instead?')

Play plan: Where is it?

Name: ....   Key person: ....

Area of Learning: CLL   Focus: Language for communication   Individual target: Ask and answer simple 'where?' questions

Glue a mirror to the bottom of a small box. As it is passed around at circle time, ask each child to take a peep inside and tell you something special they see there. Ask 'Where's ☺?'

Arrange a collection of small boxes on a table and, each session, place miniature objects in different boxes. Ask ☺ 'where's the car?'

Each day, hide the group's mascot in a different place and challenge ☺ and the other children to find it, asking 'where?' questions as you do so.

Look for lift-the-flap books and use these to reinforce 'where?' questions.

Help ☺ to select what to play with next and then ask where he or she wants to play with it. Emphasise the 'where' with a taught sign and look at ☺ expectantly.

Play a version of hide and seek with a group. Ask everyone to stay hidden until you call them, let ☺ be the seeker and then ask ☺ where each child is hiding as they are called back.

Play repetitive hiding games with cushions, blankets or upturned boxes: 'Where is Moggie? Here is Moggie!'

Teach a 'where?' sign. Hold your hands up in front of your body with palms up and horizontal. Circle them anticlockwise (left hand) and clockwise (right hand). Look expectantly with your face and ask 'where?' at the same time.

Dip in

Play plan: A nice gesture

Name: ....   **Key person:** ....

Area of Learning: CLL   **Focus: Language for communication**   **Individual target: Use gestures to clarify what is being said**

If ☺'s speech is very unclear, introduce a choice board of photographs so that ☺ can use pointing to indicate what to do next or who to play with.

Introduce a few simple signs that ☺ can use to make certain words more clear to understand. For example, there is a reference to Makaton on page 8.

Play musical instruments together and invent signals and gestures that a 'conductor' can use to control everyone's playing.

Teach ☺ how to point. At first, ask ☺ to point to a chosen toy, then point to something yourself and ask ☺ to look at it or fetch it for you.

Play miming games during circle time. One child comes into the centre of the circle and pretends to do something without speaking. The rest guess what is happening.

Model gesture yourself as you speak to ☺. Use your arms, your hands, your whole facial expression and body language to make your meaning clearer.

Share action rhymes together so that ☺ practises combining voice with gestures.

Use role-play to introduce different gestures and to practise these together – for example, how to signal that you are tired and need to go to bed. Try signalling to each other across the yard!

Language for Thinking

CLL

Language disorders may affect the way that children process and sequence their language and can therefore affect the way that these children think and process information.

▲ ● ■ Links to Area of Learning

The speech and language that you actually observe from a child is a little like the peak of an iceberg. As well as the sounds, words, gestures, tones of voice and body language that you can hear or see, there are the thoughts, vocabulary and sequences of ideas represented in the way that language structures are laid down within the brain. When you consider this, you can begin to appreciate that many children who have speech and language difficulties will also have some weaknesses in the way they think. For example, some children find that grammatical structure does not flow easily for them (a syntactic difficulty), others find the meanings of words hard to grasp (a semantic difficulty) and others still find it hard to find the right words from their memories (a word retrieval difficulty). This is why we have included activities in this book for encouraging thinking skills inchildren who have speech and language development.

Most young children soon begin to understand and respond to the different things said to them in a familiar context by familiar people. They do this by making links in their thinking between the spoken word, what is happening at the time, what happens next and what they see, touch or sense. The multi-sensory nature of the experience makes it possible to form all these links. For children who have any kind of processing weakness, your role becomes one of making language learning and development as multi-sensory as possible; new language experiences should be linked to real objects, real actions, and a whole wealth of information from the situation, your own expressions and body language as well as your expectations. This form of 'total communication' allows children with difficulties to make links even when they find it hard to remember words alone.

Use your talk to help the child connect ideas and experiences, accompanying this with real illustrations and demonstrations where possible. Show children ideas as well as telling them. Look for concrete or visual ways to help children sequence and order their thoughts and ideas or to reflect on the past and the future. Never assume that a child with language difficulties will be making these links automatically in their thinking – instead, plan activities and experiences that will bring this home for them. Concepts (such as full/empty, many/few, happy/sad) are the building blocks of thinking and you will need to be on the alert for vocabulary and concepts that are missing. You can then plan experiences for the child to be introduced to new words and language and to generalise it to new situations.

▲ ● ■ Assessment records

You will find an assessment record for working out which skills and competencies the child has already acquired on the next two pages. As a starting point, look out for and work on behaviours that are sometimes demonstrated.

Assessment sheet: Language for Thinking

Name: .... Key person: ....

Communication, Language and Literacy

Language for Communication and Thinking: Language for Thinking

enter date observed

Development matters	What I do now	Never	Sometimes	Always
Sending out messages	Stop shouting or crying when an adult approaches			
	Call out to an adult			
	Use appropriate sounds to attract your attention			
Receiving messages	Turn when my name is said			
	Look at a familiar object/person when it is named			
First spoken thoughts	Use words to attract your attention*			
	Say 'yes' and 'no'			
	Tell you something that is happening out of your view			
	Recount a simple experience*			
	Tell you how I feel			
Linking actions with words	Follow a simple gesture or sign (for example, a sign for 'no')			
	Use a few action words (for example, singing/running)*			
	Follow a simple one-step request			
	Follow a simple two-step request (first this, then that)			
Learning concepts	Can show you the big/small one when you ask me			
	Can identify four basic colours when you ask me to			
	Can tell you which is long/short			

Language to explain
- Can name six colours when playing*
- Can talk about high/low, heavy/light, happy/sad
- Link cause with effect ('because I fell over')
- Talk about an idea I have had
- Give simple directions to others*
- 'Think out loud' when problem-solving

Talking and imagining
- Talk about the here and now
- Talk through a puppet or small-world character
- Use language during role-play
- Use talk to pretend imaginary situations

Learning from experience
- Know when to ask an adult for help
- Explain the routine of the group to another
- Give a simple explanation about why something is happening
- Retell a simple story heard previously*
- Reflect on the past
- Talk about the future events

Early Learning Goals:

Use language to imagine and recreate roles and experiences.
Use talk to organise, sequence and clarify thinking, ideas, feelings and events.

▲ ● ■ Look, listen and note

Here are some of the things to look out for, especially with children who have speech and language difficulties.

• Observe the way in which young children show you that they have understood you. Was it your words that they were paying attention to, or was it the context, your actions and your non-verbal behaviour (facial expression, tone of voice, and so on)?

• Look out for jargon words – words that the child has made up to represent things, people or actions. Are these changed each time or are they used consistently to represent one thing?

• Note the times when the child is most likely to use language to communicate, to share, to express their ideas and to think things out. Who was there, what was happening at the time and what happened next?

• Observe how easily the child is acquiring new concepts. Observe whether the child can match (for example placing all the red cars together), identify ('show me the red one') and then label ('what colour is this one?').

• Record and then transcribe a piece of language collected during a learning experience, at home and during imaginary play. What does this tell you about the pathways to language that this child is following and how you can support it?

▲ ● ■ Effective practice

• Remember that for most children, understanding what is said comes before being able to say it his or herself. However, for some children with speech and language difficulties, the opposite is true so you should remain on the alert for the subtle signs of any comprehension difficulty.

• Play alongside the child, using your own simple language to interpret what the child is doing. Provide a running commentary about what the child is doing. This helps children to link your language to their actions.

• Do not bombard children with questions, especially if they might have a speech and language difficulty. Offer choices instead. As their language develops further, you can then begin to ask more open-ended questions to encourage greater reflection and thinking.

• Plan opportunities for children to develop their language and thinking skills by playing with and talking to each other. Look for chances to group children with others who provide good role models for language development.

• Use a plan/do/review format to help children think ahead about what they want to do, and review how it went afterwards.

• When language emerges in the wrong order or with the wrong words or sounds, simply echo back what the child would have said (correctly) if only they could have. This allows the child to hear the correct version, prevents a feeling of failure and allows other children to understand what has been said.

▲ ● ■ How to use the play plans

On pages 39–44 you will find six play plans for those skills marked with an asterisk on the assessment sheets on pages 36 and 37. Each play plan contains eight interventions that you could try. There are also two blank spaces to add your own personalised interventions onto each play plan.

Dip in

Play plan: I'm calling

Area of Learning: CLL

Name: ....

Key person: ....

Focus: Language for thinking

Individual target: Use words to attract your attention

Consider a picture exchange system in which ☺ hands you a card with a symbol or picture on in order to ask for something. Say the word as you accept the card. There is a reference to PECS on page 8.

If a favourite child or adult comes into the room, help ☺ shout to that person and make sure it attracts attention 'Gemma listen, ☺ is calling you!'

Teach a simple sign for 'drink' or 'teddy' and help ☺ to shape the sign before handing that thing over. Always say the word as you sign.

Sing a favourite action song with ☺ (such as bouncing ☺ on your knee for 'this is the way the ladies ride') and pause between verses until ☺ vocalises for more.

For babies, make sure you stop what you are doing and respond when the baby vocalises – this will help to teach them that their sounds can be used to gain attention from others.

Find a natural way of naming everything as you play together.

Place a light chiffon scarf over ☺'s face until ☺ makes a sound and remove it with a chuckle and a 'peep-bo!' Stop if there is any distress and try again another time.

As ☺ begins to make simple sounds, provide the first sound to start ☺ off. For example, if ☺ wants the ball, say 'b...,' as you hold up the ball and encourage ☺ to say the word.

Sequential

Play plan: What's going on?

Name: ....

Key person: ....

Area of Learning: CLL   Focus: Language for thinking

Individual target: Recount a simple experience

1 At first, simply relate what has happened to the child using your whole tone of voice and expression and making sure that ☺ is watching your face. For example, 'Look. ☺ got very wet!'

2 At a later stage, rephrase what you are saying as a question, using the same expression and tone and waiting for a yes/no response. For example, 'Oh dear! Did you get very wet?'

3 When ☺ is understanding a little more, ask 'What happened?', encouraging ☺ to show you through actions or gestures what happened. Add simple words for ☺ to hear – for example, 'Oh – you got wet!'

4 When something exciting has happened, encourage ☺ to 'tell' you what is going on. Pretend not to know about it so that ☺ works hard to make it clear.

5 Pass a treasure box around at circle time and help ☺ find a few words to describe what is in the box.

6 Ask parents to provide some photographs of a happy family event and use these as a talking point in the setting.

7 Review with ☺ how the session has gone and what the best parts were. What will ☺ do tomorrow?

8 Make up a photograph book of ☺ playing and place it in the book corner. Other children will enjoy sharing it with ☺ and talking about what went on.

Play plan: A piece of the action!

Name: .... Key person: ....

Area of Learning: CLL   Focus: Language for thinking   Individual target: Use a few action words (for example, singing/running)

Sing action rhymes during music circle time that involve simple action words and encourage looking and listening (see photocopiable page 91 for an example).

Present ☺ with some photographs showing him or her doing different things. Ask ☺ to 'Show me the one where ☺ is running' or 'Show me ☺ singing' (and so on).

Ask questions that encourage ☺ to think and talk and to use action words. For example, 'What's happening?' or 'Now what?'

Make up some digital photographs of different activities in your setting and offer ☺ choices – for example, 'Painting next or playing outside?'

Play a circle game in which children swap places across the circle to an action that you give them (for example, 'crawling').

As ☺ plays, provide a very simple commentary about ☺'s actions – for example, 'Now ☺ is crawling.'

When you give ☺ a simple direction, pause to see whether ☺ responds to words alone before showing ☺ what to do, repeating the action word as you do so.

Use puppet play or small-world play to introduce and reinforce new action rhymes. Keep it fun and relaxed and involve other children too.

Dip in

Play plan: Fun with colour

Name: .... Key person: ....

Area of Learning: CLL Focus: Language for thinking

Individual target: Can name six colours when playing

Set up a game in the home corner with coloured cups, saucers and plates. Use soft toys and puppets to 'ask' ☺ what colour their cups are.

Enjoy the dressing-up clothes with a small group of children and use this as a natural opportunity for identifying and naming colours with ☺.

Spend some time helping ☺ to identify colours by playing naturally together and asking ☺ to pass you, for example, some craft materials ('☺ pass me the blue piece please').

Set up a colour table and challenge each child to place something red, blue and so on, upon it. Use it as a talking point with ☺.

Make up some coloured cards with black one side and colour the other. Place them upside down on the floor and challenge ☺ to turn them over one at a time and call out the colour.

Make sure that ☺ can match colours during free play and during structured activities before you ask ☺ to identify or name colours.

Use favourite toys (such as Thomas the Tank engine) to reinforce colours. For example, keep repeating, 'James is the red engine.' Later, help ☺ make links; 'It's the colour of James! What colour is James?'

Use these activities (among others) to talk to ☺ about colours: mixing play dough, icing biscuits, playing with coloured water, using coloured paper to paint on and sorting out the construction bricks.

■SCHOLASTIC
www.scholastic.co.uk

Play plan: This is the way...

Name: ....

Key person: ....

Area of Learning: CLL   Focus: Language for thinking

Individual target: Give simple directions to others.

Give ☺ a special job to do in order to help you ('Ask the children to come inside now, please').

Ask ☺ to show and tell another child how to make a model or a picture just like ☺'s.

Give ☺ something to pass to another child ('☺, take this box to Freya, please').

After ☺ has enjoyed or achieved something really special, ask ☺ to dictate to you while you write down a story all about what ☺ did.

Set up a puppet theatre and encourage ☺ to direct what the puppets do from the front. Offer choices at first and keep it simple ('Shall we use Sooty or Sweep next?').

Give ☺ a magic wand at circle time. Ask ☺ to tell all the children what to do and then wave the wand! Let everyone have a turn.

When you notice ☺ at a loss for a word to direct others, offer a choice of words to use (for example 'excuse me', 'can I play?' or 'let me pass please').

Suggest that one child becomes a robot while ☺ tells them what to do. Offer your support and encouragement, especially with position words such as forwards/backwards.

Dip in

Play plan: Tell me a story

Area of Learning: CLL **Focus: Language for thinking**

Name: .... **Key person:** ....

Individual target: Retell a simple story heard previously

Share a story with ☺ first before you share it with the whole group. Ask ☺ to tell the other children a little bit about the book before you read it to everyone.

Break a story down in small chunks and ask ☺ to tell you about each little part as you record ☺'s words onto tape or mini CD. Then string ☺'s words together into a whole recorded story for all the children to listen to as ☺ turns the pages.

Ask ☺ to retell a simple story to you while you draw a simple picture sequence. Then help ☺ to use that picture sequence to retell the story to another child.

Help ☺ to make up a simple picture book for the book corner and then share it with other children as ☺ retells the story.

Encourage ☺ to 'read' familiar picture books to the soft toys or the puppets.

When you read a familiar story at group time, pause before the repetitive refrains for ☺ and the others to join in.

Start with a really familiar story. Ask ☺ what happens on the next page.

Make up some simple picture cards about a family story and ask ☺ to arrange these in order afterwards. Start with just three cards to sequence and gradually build this up.

Linking Sounds and Letters

Children who have difficulties in forming sounds may find it hard to link sounds to letters, though there is plenty you can do to enable them to make progress.

▲ ● ■ Links to Area of Learning

There is some research that links early speech and language difficulties to a greater risk of specific learning difficulties, such as dyslexia, later on. It makes sense to be aware of this risk and to compensate by making early learning as multi-sensory as possible for all the children. From the earliest age, most babies are learning to listen to, distinguish and respond to intonations and the sound of voices. In time, this develops into the ability to distinguish between different letter sounds. The babbling stage enjoyed by almost all children shows that they are already repeating certain sounds more then others and beginning to see patterns in them. Most children then begin to experiment with using sounds and words to represent the objects and people around them. They begin to show a real interest in word patterns and enjoy songs and rhymes. It is at this stage that they begin to repeat common phrases in stories and in familiar situations.

Some children with speech and language difficulties have problems in distinguishing between different letter sounds and seeing patterns in them. Even though their hearing might be fine, they have not laid down the neural pathways in their brains that help them to discriminate between sounds fluently and effectively. Perhaps they also have difficulty in sequencing these sounds to form words, either because of the way their language processing works or because they have difficulties coordinating their mouth and tongue movements. All this means that it is perfectly possible to teach the link between sounds and letters but that it might take specific attention and targeting on your part. The play plans in this section should help you to do this.

Although this book does not focus on children with hearing difficulties, it is interesting to note that these children may not go through a babbling phase because they may not be able to distinguish between sounds. You might have noticed other young children in your care who become quiet when they have colds or who suddenly begin to vocalise and speak more clearly once they have had grommets inserted – these are the children who have intermittent ear infections and glue ear. The middle ear becomes congested with sticky mucus so that sounds do not transmit easily and the insertion of a tiny tube (or 'grommet') helps the ear chamber to drain. Many of the activities in this section will be helpful for these children too. As usual, you should adapt the play plans flexibly in light of what you know about the individual children and their needs.

▲ ● ■ Assessment records

You will find an assessment record for working out which skills and competencies the child has already acquired on the next two pages. As a starting point, look out for, and work on behaviours that are sometimes demonstrated.

Assessment sheet: Linking Sounds and Letters

Name:............................ Key person:.............

Communication, Language and Literacy

Communication, Language and Literacy: Linking Sounds and Letters

enter date observed

Development matters	What I do now	Never	Sometimes	Always
Distinguishing sounds	Turn to look at familiar voices			
	Look happy when you use a happy tone			
	Turn expectantly to the sounds of dinner being prepared*			
Sound patterns	Repeat strings of sounds with my voice			
	Respond to music with a sing-song tone of voice			
	Repeat actions that create sounds (such as beating a drum)			
	Clap hands in an action rhyme			
Copying rhythms	Copy two or three beats on a drum*			
	Copy a fast or a slow hand clap			
	Join in simple action rhymes			
	March to a beat			
	Clap the syllables in familiar words with help			
Speaking fluently	Speak sounds on first attempt without stuttering*			
	Regulate the speed of my speech so others can understand me			
	Express myself adequately even if excited or distressed			
Enjoying rhyme	Enjoy listening to songs and rhymes			
	Join in with some repetitive rhyming words			

Word sounds	
	Suggest rhyming words for an ending*
	Spot words that do not rhyme
	Tell you what sound an object begins with (note which sounds)
	Show you something beginning with 't' and so on (note which sounds)
	Find you a 't' (and so on) from a string of letters (note which sounds)
	Link written letters to pictures of familiar objects (note which sounds)
	Tell you which letter sound an object ends with (note which sounds)*
Identify middle sounds	
	Early word building
	Recognise some of the letters in my name
	Make an attempt to write my name*
	Make an attempt to read and write regular CVC words

Early Learning Goals:

Hear and say sounds in words in the order in which they occur.
Link sounds to letters, naming and sounding the letters of the alphabet.
Use their phonic knowledge to write simple, regular words and make phonetically plausible attempts at more complex words.

▲ ● ■ Look, listen and note

These are the observations that will be particularly useful for children who have difficulties in discriminating and remembering sounds.

• Be alert to the range of sounds that a baby is making. If you feel that these are limited or unusual, this might be your first sign that hearing needs checking.

• Watch for babies and young children's reactions to the familiar sounds around them. Do they turn to anticipate what is happening?

• Observe how well a child pays attention to sounds. Do they listen to you when you call them? Do they behave differently when they hear certain sounds? How are their listening skills coming on (note down your evidence)?

• Observe how the child responds at music and rhyme time. Is any attention paid to the words themselves? Is there any sign of rhythm and rhyme developing? Is there any attempt yet to join in with voice?

• Look at the child's early attempts to read and mark-make – is there any evidence that they recognise or know a few letter sounds, such as those in their own name?

• Do early attempts at decoding CVC words appear to be logical and typical of how children usually learn? In other words, are they beginning to link letters and sounds in a consistent way?

▲ ● ■ Effective practice

• Create quiet spaces where you can listen to sounds, identify them and talk about them together.

• Direct a young child's attention before a listening task or speaking with them.

• Draw attention to sounds around you – some of the children might not have noticed them. Do not have 'blanket' background music playing as this encourages the children to ignore sounds.

• Hold a regular musical circle time with rhymes, action songs and musical activities to encourage listening skills, rhythm and rhyme. Don't be afraid to have fun – this will boost everybody's confidence and motivation!

• When listening to and experimenting with letter sounds, keep the activity multi-sensory (looking, listening, doing) and over-emphasise the sounds you are focusing on (for example, 'fish' 'sheep', 'coat'!). Some multi-sensory schemes combine sounds with actions or pictures.

• Use magnetic letters when you first introduce letter sounds so that they can be handled as well as seen and spoken. Another very tactile method is to use a shallow dry sand tray and trace letters with your fingertips.

• Keep any activities with letters at this stage enjoyable and unthreatening. Children with difficulties will be quickly put off if activities become too formal too quickly. Make sure that each and every child can feel success at whatever level they are capable of.

• Make books and storytelling an integral part of your setting so that children's early experiences of reading and letter sounds are enjoyable and enriching.

▲ ● ■ How to use the play plans

On pages 49–54 you will find six play plans for those skills marked with an asterisk on the assessment sheets on pages 46 and 47. Each play plan contains eight interventions that you could try. There are two blank spaces to add your own personalised interventions onto each play plan.

Dip in

Play plan: Listen well

Area of Learning: CLL   Focus: Linking sounds and letters   Individual target: Turn expectantly to the sounds of dinner being prepared

Name: ....   Key person: ....

When you bring out a noisy toy that ☺ loves to play with regularly, make the sound first (before ☺ sees the toy) and encourage ☺ to turn to look for it.

Hide a shaking rattle momentarily from view and then share ☺'s fun as it reappears. For older babies, play with feely bags in which you have hidden noise-making toys and instruments.

Encourage all staff members to use ☺'s name before speaking, in order to engage attention and encourage listening skills.

Try your best to cut down on the number of times adults enter and leave nursery rooms (some rooms can feel like busy corridors – this is noisy and distracting for babies!).

Record a series of everyday sounds onto a CD or tape and play a game in which you match sounds to real objects or pictures of objects.

For a very young baby, always use the same soft, sing-song tones as you approach so that ☺ can begin to distinguish and recognise each of your voices.

Draw ☺'s attention to the sounds of your daily routine – the dinner plates coming in, the rain outside or another baby laughing in the paddling pool.

If you hear a fire engine, aeroplane or big truck outside, hold ☺ up to the window to see it passing by.

Sequential

Play plan: Can you hear the beat?   Name: ....

Area of Learning: CLL   Focus: Linking sounds and letters

Key person: ....

Individual target: Copy two or three beats on a drum

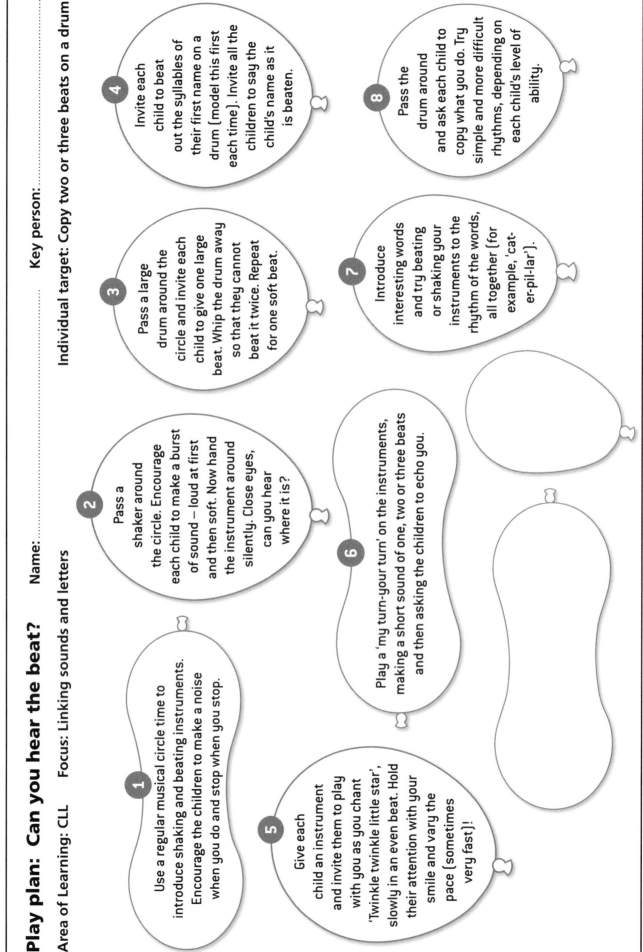

4 Invite each child to beat out the syllables of their first name on a drum (model this first each time). Invite all the children to say the child's name as it is beaten.

8 Pass the drum around and ask each child to copy what you do. Try simple and more difficult rhythms, depending on each child's level of ability.

3 Pass a large drum around the circle and invite each child to give one large beat. Whip the drum away so that they cannot beat it twice. Repeat for one soft beat.

7 Introduce interesting words and try beating or shaking your instruments to the rhythm of the words, all together (for example, 'cat-er-pil-lar').

2 Pass a shaker around the circle. Encourage each child to make a burst of sound – loud at first and then soft. Now hand the instrument around silently. Close eyes, can you hear where it is?

6 Play a 'my turn-your turn' on the instruments, making a short sound of one, two or three beats and then asking the children to echo you.

1 Use a regular musical circle time to introduce shaking and beating instruments. Encourage the children to make a noise when you do and stop when you stop.

5 Give each child an instrument and invite them to play with you as you chant 'Twinkle twinkle little star', slowly in an even beat. Hold their attention with your smile and vary the pace (sometimes very fast)!

PHOTOCOPIABLE

Dip in

Play plan: TALKING NATURALLY

Name: ....   Key person: ....

Area of Learning: CLL   Focus: Linking sounds and letters   Individual target: Speak sounds on first attempt without stuttering

Poor sleep and feeling generally unwell can cause stammering to become worse – keep in touch with parents and carers and try to ensure that ☺ has a good night's sleep.

When ☺ talks to you, give ☺ your full attention and do not interrupt.

Try to keep your own language at ☺'s level and keep your rate of speaking slow. This might help ☺ to feel more relaxed about speaking.

Try not to confront ☺ with the need to speak (for example, 'Tell Amy what you did'). Instead look for chances to talk together naturally, perhaps sharing a plaything or activity.

Try to arrange five to ten minutes each session when you can be together quietly with ☺ (and one or two other children) to share a story or play quietly in a relaxed situation.

If ☺ stutters or stammers, never complete what ☺ is trying to say. Look interested and wait patiently. See photocopiable page 92 for tips on dealing with dysfluency – print copies for colleagues, parents and carers.

Don't correct ☺'s speech if mistakes are made (such as 'dod' for 'dog'). Instead, model the correct pronunciation afterwards.

Cut down on direct questions. Instead, keep the conversation natural. For example, 'I bet you enjoyed your dinner today' would be less threatening than 'What did you eat for dinner today?'

■ SCHOLASTIC
www.scholastic.co.uk

Dip in

Play plan: First rhymes

Area of Learning: CLL   **Focus: Linking sounds and letters**

Name: ....

Key person: ....

Individual target: Suggest rhyming words for an ending

In a small group, chant a favourite rhyme to ☺ and leave out the last word of each line or verse for ☺ to complete.

Challenge the children to find toy objects for a rhyming box. For example, it could have a frog, a dog, a cog and a log. Support ☺ by over-emphasising the sounds.

Introduce a new rhyme and try just saying the first sound of the last word. See whether ☺ can come in with the rest. For example, 'One, two, buckle my sh...'

Make a picture book with ☺. Choose a rhyming string such as '-at' and make a picture of an '-at' word (such as cat, hat, mat) on each page. Emphasise the rhymes as you turn the pages.

Make up a new rhyme and help ☺ to find alternative words for the endings that rhyme. For example, 'When I was one, I .....' (ate a bun/had some fun/went for a run, and so on).

Share nursery rhymes, songs and action rhymes on a daily basis. Look for a balance between songs to listen to and songs to make actions to, as young children cannot do both at once.

Invite the children to make up a silly rhyme (that they feel comfortable with) about their name – for example, 'Rosie Posie', 'Liam Triam' and 'Ben Again'.

Put out a selection of items such as a cup, a ball and a toy cat. Ask ☺ to find 'the one that sounds like lup' and so on.

Sequential

Play plan: What do I end with?

Area of Learning: CLL

Name: ....

Key person: ....

Focus: Linking sounds and letters

Individual target: Tell you which letter sound an object ends with

1 Make sure that ☺ is secure on hearing most initial sounds before moving on to a few end sounds.

2 Play a game with a mumbling puppet who only says the last sound clearly. Ask ☺ what the puppet is asking for from a choice of two objects – '....n' for the car or the train?

3 Now help ☺ to speak for the mumbling puppet and ask another child to guess. Keep it fun and light-hearted.

4 Adapt the game so that there is a greater choice and try introducing pictures of objects instead of the real things.

5 Introduce a new version of 'I spy' at circle time: 'I hear with my little ear, something that ends with ....'. Arrange additional support for ☺ in order to focus attention on the last sound and to model possible answers.

6 Give ☺ a shopping bag and help ☺ move around the room collecting things that end with a given letter sound.

7 Introduce the letter shape (use tactile letters embossed with sandpaper or magnetic letters) to all of these activities so that you are hearing the sound, looking at the shape and handling the letter simultaneously.

8 Select a series of pictures representing regular and familiar words (such as dog, ball, jug, cup, cat). Challenge ☺ to tell you which letter each one ends with.

Sequential

Play plan: Writing my name

Name: ....

Key person: ....

Area of Learning: CLL   Focus: Linking sounds and letters

Individual target: Make an attempt to write my name

1. Provide themed areas with writing paper and mark-making tools – such as a post office. Balance times when ☺ plays there freely with time when you support and encourage ☺ in early mark-making.

2. Hold ☺'s hand as you help ☺ trace the first letter of ☺'s name in the dry sand tray. Use your own finger to trace the rest of the name.

3. Use hand-over-hand to help ☺ for the first letter of ☺'s name on paintings, models and so on. Use your own writing to print the remaining letters.

4. Continue for a while at this level, gradually helping ☺ to add more letters to ☺'s name.

5. Reinforce the circular movements involved in writing by playing with ribbons and streamers. Trace figures of eight (on their sides) in the air using huge movements from one side of the body to the other.

6. Write ☺'s name in large yellow felt-tipped pen onto a sheet of paper and invite ☺ to trace over it.

7. Offer hand-over-hand so that ☺ becomes used to the whole hand and wrist movement involved in forming the letters. Sound out each letter as you write it.

8. Give ☺ a name card to copy beneath. Make a huge fuss when ☺ makes any attempt, however immature, to write his or her name independently.

Responding to Experiences

CD

Children who have speech and language difficulties can quickly become frustrated as they try to put their meaning across. In this chapter you will find some strategies to help them respond to and share their experiences with others.

▲●■ Links to Area of Learning

Sometimes the first sign of a speech and language difficulty is the frustration that certain children show when they are dealing with experiences and trying to communicate what they want to others. If children lack the words to express themselves clearly, they can become either cross with the world or reluctant to continue to try – both patterns of behaviour are typical. It is one of the most rewarding aspects of early years teaching when you are able to help a child to communicate more clearly and you witness the dramatic change in behaviour and confidence that this can bring.

In the early stages, most babies respond to experiences with movement; in time reaching out for and using their various senses to explore objects further. In this way they begin to respond to what they see, hear, feel, touch and smell. They express themselves through physical play and the sounds that they make and they also repeat patterns of play as if enjoying and wishing to consolidate any new way of playing. So far, children with speech and language difficulties will behave no differently to other children. However, from around the age of two, most children are beginning to use their early words and language to speak about and begin to make sense of their experiences. They use language and other forms of communication to share the things that they create or to indicate their excitement or frustration. Here, the child whose language is not developing along the usual pathway might be at a disadvantage and need your additional support. Your role becomes one of encouraging them to continue to use all their senses to explore and create and to find ways of helping them express themselves as clearly as possible to others. For some children, this involves planning alternative ways for the child to communicate what they feel (for example using feelings boards, gestures and signs, presenting choices, using careful observations). For others, it is a matter of keeping experiences as multi-sensory as possible, using your own words and commentaries to help the child link the language to the experience.

For all children, you need to enter into dialogue about their creations and experiences, keeping your language and pace at the appropriate level for a particular child to respond to. Children need to find ways of getting across to others what they were trying to do; as well as finding ways to look back on how their experiences turned out – this can be hard for a child who cannot manage verb tenses, but nevertheless possible for you to interpret. The best rule of thumb is to listen to what children are saying to you (and not how they say it), and to respond accordingly.

▲●■ Assessment records

You will find an assessment record for working out which skills and competencies the child has already acquired on the next two pages. As a starting point look, out for and work on behaviours that are sometimes demonstrated.

Assessment sheet: Being Creative – Responding to Experiences   Name: ....   Key person: ....

Communication, Language and Literacy   Communication, Language and Literacy: Creative Development: Responding to experiences

Development matters	What I do now	Never	Sometimes enter date observed	Always
Respond to experiences with movement	Move more when you approach			
	Kick and wave my arms to music*			
	Move my whole body when excited			
Respond to experiences with touch	Wave arms when a toy is held near me			
	Swipe at toys and vocalise			
	Grasp toys and explore them with taste and touch			
Respond to experiences with voice	Vocalise happily when in company			
	Shout out happily to another adult or child			
	Share laughter and giggles with others			
	Use my voice to indicate that I want to join in*			
Indicate 'more'	Use eye-contact to signal 'more please'			
	Vocalise to signal 'more please'			
	Nod when you ask 'more?' or 'again?'			
Ask for 'more'	Share play experiences with others			
	Look up at you while playing			
	Pass a toy to you while playing			
	Watch others play and imitate*			
	Babble or talk to another child while playing alongside			
	Ask if I can play			
	Chatter easily to others as we play together			

Use words to express likes and dislikes	Turn away from an unwanted food item or toy				
	Indicate 'no' through my actions				
	Indicate yes/no				
	Say 'yes' and 'no'				
	Say what I like and what I don't like				
Tell you what I want to do next	My free play makes it clear what I want to do				
	I can point or pull you towards what I want to do				
	Choose between two activities offered to me				
	Choose my next activity using a choice or feelings board*				
Talk about how I feel	Indicate how I feel through my behaviour and expressions				
	Use a few feelings words appropriately				
	Complete a feelings sentence during circle time*				
	Talk about past experiences				
	Talk about past photographs				
Share an item of news	Tell you what made me upset				
	Talk about when I was little				
	Talk about future experiences				
	Talk about what we will do tomorrow*				
Share a future holiday/trip	Tell you what is making me feel excited				
	Talk about when I am older				

Early Learning Goals:

Respond in a variety of ways to what they see, hear, smell, touch and feel.

▲ ● ■ Look, listen and note

Your best way of monitoring how children respond to their early years' experiences is through regular observation. Here are some points to look out for especially with children who have (or are at risk of) speech and language difficulties or delay.

• Observe whether babies accompany their hand, leg and arm movements by vocalising more at the same time. Is it easy to tell from this how they are feeling?

• Listen to the sounds that children make as they meet different experiences. Do they make tuneful sounds as they move, or 'talk' to themselves as they play? What activities make them more vocal?

• Look for sounds and action patterns that are repeated for the pure pleasure of doing so. Is there any evidence that the child is 'playing' with new speech sounds or early words?

• Note down the first occasion when a child looks at you or calls to you in order to share an experience. What was going on at the time? What did the child say or do? Was the communicative intent clear even if the words and language were not?

• Keep examples or photographs of creations and note down what the child felt about it at the time. Revisit these photographs in order to talk about the past.

▲ ● ■ Effective practice

• Balance noisy, lively times with quiet, calm times so that you have opportunities for reflecting, listening and relaxing as well as moving about and doing things.

• Appoint a key person to tune in to how the child expresses feelings (even if the child has no spoken language) in order to communicate these ways to others.

• For children who are non-verbal, consider making a 'child passport' with photographs of the child expressing different feelings and an explanation of what is going on (for example 'This is me when I am bored. Please offer me a choice of what to do next'). For some children, their behavioural expressions may not be obvious to those who do not know the child well. Parents and carers are usually brilliant at helping you here.

• Use every method in your repertoire for making a child's first attempts to communicate their feelings to you as successful and comfortable as possible; give your time, your whole interest, your reassurance and your encouragement.

• You might have noticed that a child is most vocal with certain playthings or resources. Use this in your planning to set up small-group activities that will encourage that child to share experiences with others.

• If a child cannot cope with speaking in a large group, set up smaller groups that are less formal as a starting point.

▲ ● ■ How to use the play plans

On pages 59–64 you will find six play plans for those skills marked with an asterisk on the assessment sheets on pages 56 and 57. Each play plan contains eight interventions that you could try. There are also two blank spaces to add your own personalised interventions onto each play plan.

Dip in

Play plan: Time for music

Name: ....   Key person: ....

Area of Learning: CD

Focus: Responding to experiences   **Individual target: Kick and wave my arms to music**

Hold ☺ still on your knee as someone else starts and stops some music. When the music plays, 'dance' ☺ about on your knee and stop still when it is quiet.

Begin to use different music to signal different kinds of movement and action from the baby. For example, invent your own 'time to change the nappy' song.

Try a lively movement rhyme as you bounce ☺ on your knee. Pause to see whether ☺ begins to bounce again to indicate 'again!'

Use very calm music or a soft musical mobile to signal 'rest time' to the babies. Keep all voices low and calm. Try some lively music as the baby wakes up and gets ready to play.

Encourage parents and carers to join in too. Have the babies on play mats with the adults sitting around them in a circle. Sing a mixture of lively and quiet tunes as the babies kick their legs.

Cradle ☺ in your arms looking up at your face. Gently stroke and move ☺'s arms as you sing and smile.

Keep background music to a minimum and save it for a special music time when all the babies are alert. Regular sessions will help children vulnerable to language delay to tune in to and discriminate between sounds.

Give older babies a rattle each and encourage them to stop when the music stops by holding their hands gently and smiling in anticipation. Adapt the rhyme on page 91 to 'We shake and we shake and we STOP!'

Dip in

Play plan: Can I join in?

Name: ....   Key person: ....

Area of Learning: CD   Focus: Responding to experiences   Individual target: Use my voice to indicate that I want to join in

Play a calling out game outside. Shout something simple to ☺ (such as, 'Hey!') and roll a ball towards ☺. Encourage ☺ to shout back and push the ball away again. Continue, taking turns.

When you set out the playthings out of doors, encourage ☺ to watch from the window. When ☺ begins to call out in excitement, say, 'You want to go outside!' and let ☺ move out to play.

Help ☺ to decide what to play with next. Encourage ☺ to use voice to attract the attention of the children already playing and then explain to the children that ☺ wants to join in too.

Play a repetitive action game with ☺ sitting on your knee (such as 'round and round the garden'). Pause between verses and wait for ☺ to make a sound before repeating. Keep it fun.

Help ☺ rehearse the words to say to a group of children when ☺ wants to join in their game. Watch and support until the play gets going.

Set out some favourite playthings just out of reach of ☺. When ☺ begins to make happy sounds, say '☺ wants to play too!' and bring the toys closer.

Sit with ☺ and watch some children play. Talk about what they are doing. When ☺ vocalises and makes movements towards the playing, move ☺ into the group, saying '☺ wants to play too!'

Role-play with a puppet. Ask ☺ to call out to the puppet in order to gain the puppet's attention. Then arrange for the puppet to play with ☺.

Sequential

Play plan: I can do it too!

Area of Learning: CD   **Focus: Responding to experiences**

Name: ....   Key person: ....

Individual target: Watch others play and imitate

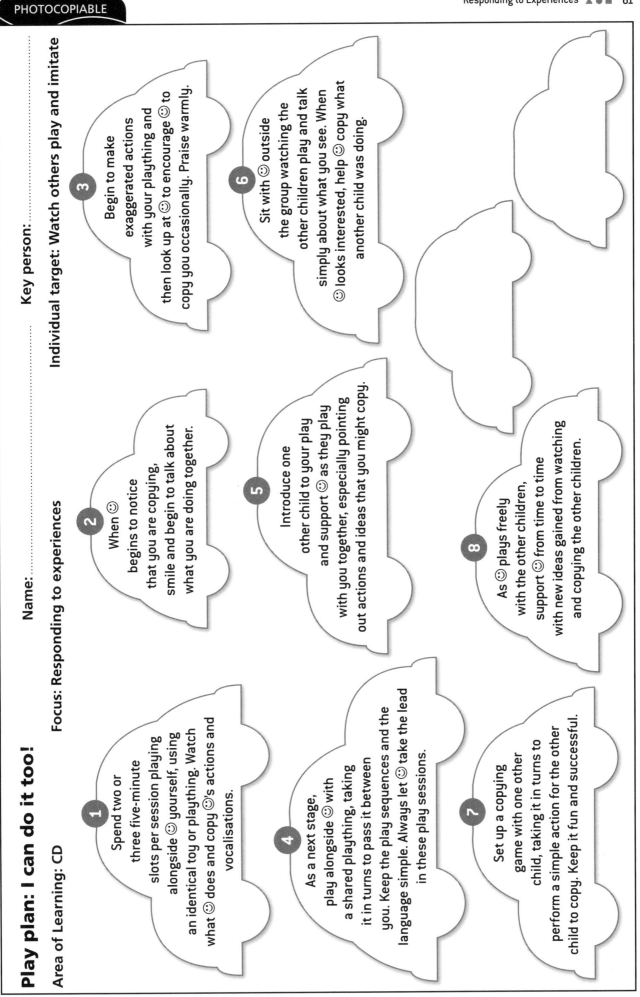

1 Spend two or three five-minute slots per session playing alongside ☺ yourself, using an identical toy or plaything. Watch what ☺ does and copy ☺'s actions and vocalisations.

2 When ☺ begins to notice that you are copying, smile and begin to talk about what you are doing together.

3 Begin to make exaggerated actions with your plaything and then look up at ☺ to encourage ☺ to copy you occasionally. Praise warmly.

4 As a next stage, play alongside ☺ with a shared plaything, taking it in turns to pass it between you. Keep the play sequences and the language simple. Always let ☺ take the lead in these play sessions.

5 Introduce one other child to your play and support ☺ as they play with you together, especially pointing out actions and ideas that you might copy.

6 Sit with ☺ outside the group watching the other children play and talk simply about what you see. When ☺ looks interested, help ☺ copy what another child was doing.

7 Set up a copying game with one other child, taking it in turns to perform a simple action for the other child to copy. Keep it fun and successful.

8 As ☺ plays freely with the other children, support ☺ from time to time with new ideas gained from watching and copying the other children.

Play plan: Time to choose

Name: ....

Area of Learning: CD   **Focus: Responding to experiences**

Individual target: Choose my next activity using a choice or feelings board

Key person: ....

Use a similar feelings board for ☺ to indicate how a particular activity went. For example, did ☺ like it or not like it? Talk about why, keeping your language simple.

Take photographs of an activity that ☺ is really enjoying. Help ☺ put the photographs into order later on and talk about the experience within a small group.

Use smaller versions on cards that can be mounted on a felt board or white board. Let ☺ use these to plan a few activities for each session, arranging cards from left to right.

Use a plan/do/ review format to help ☺ to think about what to do and how it went, by fixing simple cards onto a felt board.

Follow up your feelings board with a discussion about why ☺ is feeling that way. Is ☺ still feeling the same? What would make things different?

Set up a feelings board with four sections with simple faces on – happy, sad, cross, in-between. Ask ☺ how they are feeling today and invite ☺ to stick their name card or photograph in the right section.

Plan an activity that requires a sequence (such as making a sandwich). Sit together and plan what you need to do, drawing little picture cards for each step. Jumble them up and ask ☺ to sequence them.

Use digital photography to make a picture gallery of activities and playthings. Encourage ☺ to use pointing or words to let you know what ☺ would like to do next.

Dip in

Play plan: How I'm feeling

Name: ....

Key person: ....

Area of Learning: CD

Focus: Responding to experiences

Individual target: Complete a feelings sentence during circle time

1 Start by passing a teddy around the circle for each child in turn to tell the teddy her or his name.

2 Take a puppet around the circle asking each child a question. Keep ☺'s question simple, such as 'Do you like me?'

3 Once ☺ is confident to speak in circle time, try something more complex. Share out photographs of the children. Ask each child to say something they like about the 'person' they are holding (support ☺ by offering choices).

4 Teach the idea of sentence completion. Send this sentence around the circle, 'My name is...' Then try, 'I am...' (for example, 'three').

5 Once the children have grasped this idea, use a later session to start a feelings sentence. For example, 'I am happy when...,' or 'I like...'

6 Use a story about feelings to introduce ideas to the children. Then try a sentence 'I feel angry/ sad/scared/ happy when...'

7 Support ☺ as the sentences become more open-ended. For example, 'I feel... today because...', with each child explaining why to a puppet.

8 Break more complex sentences down for ☺, again by offering choices or asking simpler versions. Then complete the sentence for ☺ in its full form ('☺ feels worried today because he's not sure who is picking him up.')

Dip in

Play plan: Tomorrow, tomorrow

Name: ....

Key person: ....

Area of Learning: CD **Focus: Responding to experiences**

Individual target: Talk about what we will do tomorrow

Have a box that ☺ can use to put things into to represent things ☺ would like to do tomorrow – a brick for some construction, a half-finished drawing and so on.

Give ☺ a job to do relating to tomorrow's activity – something to bring from home, something to look out for on the journey home or something to prepare today for use tomorrow.

Keep photographic records of what ☺ did yesterday/last week/last year and what ☺ did today. Spend some time together wondering what ☺ will be doing tomorrow/next week/next year.

Use a group time towards the end of the session to review all the things the children have done, and plan together what they might do in the next session.

Help ☺ to review creations and activities and decide how ☺ might like to do things differently next time – such as making a blue model to go with the red one, or making an even bigger tower.

As you notice ☺ playing, move in to share the experience and ask whether ☺ would like to do something like that tomorrow as well.

Plan ahead for festivals and celebrations by talking about what you will make and do together. Start collecting resources with the children and making plans together.

If ☺ cannot speak using correct tenses, do not correct. Simply rephrase afterwards. For example, if ☺ says 'I make a big one', reply with 'Oh, you will make a bigger one!'

Expressing and Communicating Ideas

CD

Children who have speech and language difficulties may lack the words or the communication skills to express their ideas and thoughts and will need your additional support.

▲ ● ■ Links to Area of Learning

In Chapter 6, we looked at the barriers faced by children who have speech and language difficulties or delay when it comes to responding to their experiences and expressing feelings using language. How much harder it must be to use language and communication to express your thoughts and ideas to others. Thinking is an invisible process involving both visualising and also silent words. Often, a child with difficulties might be well able to visualise what he or she would like to happen next but have no idea of how to put this into words and communicate it to others. This can again lead to tremendous frustration and a feeling that one's thoughts and ideas simply do not matter. This can profoundly affect self-esteem and lead to rather quiet and withdrawn children, or very angry ones. Your role becomes one of finding the key to allow each and every child to express and communicate to others about how they are thinking and the ideas that they have. Some children will need continual support to start with, but the aim is for them to gradually be comfortable in their own way of expressing their thoughts and ideas.

In the usual pathway of development, children begin to express their thoughts and ideas to others simply by repeating actions or getting on with it and 'doing'. In time, they use representation (such as gestures and movement, art work and early mark-making) to express ideas and begin to find the words to speak them. They become more and more proficient in using language and other forms of communication to share the things that they create. They can express their ideas through music, dance, movement, painting and craft activity as well as through words. Most children can be helped to talk about their personal intentions, describing what they were trying to do. They will respond to comments and questions from yourselves or other children, entering into dialogue about their creations. They also begin to learn how to make comparisons and create new connections in their thinking and ideas.

Even at this young age, children will be developing preferences for which is the best medium to express their ideas with. Therefore, if you can offer the right choices, you should be able to find outlets for each child – whatever the level of language. In this way, all children can be helped to express and communicate their ideas, thoughts and feelings by using a widening range of materials, suitable tools, imaginative and role play, movement, designing and making, and a variety of songs and musical instruments.

▲ ● ■ Assessment records

You will find an assessment record for working out which skills and competencies the child has already acquired on the next two pages. As a starting point, look out for and work on behaviours that are sometimes, but not always, demonstrated.

Assessment sheet: Being Creative – Expressing and Communicating Ideas Name:............ Key person:............

Communication, Language and Literacy Creative Development: Expressing and Communicating Ideas

enter date observed

Development matters	What I do now	Never			Sometimes			Always		
Repeating play patterns	Reach out for a favourite toy									
	Show preferences in toys and playthings									
	Explore by repeating patterns of play*									
	Show preferences in activities									
Using representation	Move in a way that communicates excitement									
	Use gestures to represent words (such as pointing to what I want)									
	Adopt body language to represent happy/grumpy/sad*									
Enjoy painting	Sometimes say that my drawings represent something									
	Enjoy using craft and construction to make things									
Expressing ideas without words	Willing to express myself through movement									
	Willing to express myself through music*									
	Willing to express myself through dance									
	Willing to express myself through art									
Expressing ideas through words	Indicate what I want to do simply by getting on with it									
	Communicate to you what I want to do using a gestures and words									
	Share a new idea with another child using gestures and actions									
	Use words to volunteer an idea									

Speaking out

- Share a creative activity with another child
- Volunteer a simple idea during group time
- Assert myself appropriately to other children*
- Tell other children all about my creation
- Share a creative plan with another child

Discussions and questions

- Willing to answer simple questions about my creation
- Chat easily with others while creating
- Gauge what the listener already knows when discussing topics*
- Talk to another child about what they are doing
- Show interest in other children's ideas too
- Ask why/what/how questions

Making links

- Recall memories as I create and discuss
- Develop my creations in the light of what I have seen others do
- Develop my ideas in the light of what we have talked about*
- Express my ideas through role play
- Express my ideas through imaginative play and creativity
- Develop my ideas from day to day and talk about what I am doing

Early Learning Goals:

Express and communicate their ideas, thoughts and feelings by using a widening range of materials, suitable tools, imaginative and role-play, movement, designing and making, and a variety of songs and musical instruments.

▲ ● ■ Look, listen and note

Try to tune in to how children with speech and language difficulties express themselves using these kinds of observations.

• Start by observing how and where children play, making a note of how long they remain interested in an activity and what choices they make. This will give you an idea about their interests and what is important to them, even if a child cannot express this in words.

• Observe what kinds of situations children appear to be at their most relaxed or most creative. For example, are they happiest when expressing themselves through music, art, design, movement, dance or imaginative play?

• Some children with communication difficulties have unusual patterns of attention. Observe whether a child is most responsive to movement, to touch, to smell or to things to look at. Sometimes you can see this because the child behaves in a way to keep certain senses busy (for example, lining up toys in a certain way because that appearance gives them pleasure).

• Keep a note of the gestures and signs that children use and note the situations in which these are used to express themselves. Perhaps you can introduce more signs to aid language and communication? Discuss this with any speech and language therapist involved if you feel it might be a useful option.

• Note how a child combines vocalisations, movement, gestures and body language to express or communicate how they are thinking and feeling.

▲ ● ■ Effective practice

• Plan activities that include the choices and interests of the less vocal children – this makes it clear to them that their preferences and choices are important too.

• For children who do not have much language, make sure that there are always plenty of non-verbal ways of expressing their thoughts and ideas, such as through music or art.

• Always respond to the way children are expressing their ideas and thoughts even if they cannot put these into words – in other words, 'read' their behaviour, rather than expect them always to tell you things.

• Offer a wide range of choices of different resources, media and tools when a child is about to play creatively. This way, you can encourage the creativity and expression of children who might not be able to explain to you what they need or what they are aiming for.

• It might take longer than usual for a child with language difficulties to tell you about their creations. Make sure you allow yourself time to be patient and encouraging as you support the child in expressing opinions and ideas. Slow the pace down and keep your own sentences short and positive.

▲ ● ■ How to use the play plans

On pages 69–74 you will find six play plans for those skills marked with an asterisk on the assessment sheets on pages 66 and 67. Each play plan contains eight interventions that you could try. There are two blank spaces to add your own personalised interventions onto each play plan.

Dip in

Play plan: Again, again!

Focus: Expressing and Communicating Ideas

Name: ....

Area of Learning: CD

Individual target: Explore by repeating patterns of play

Key person: ....

Sit in front of a full-length mirror and encourage ☺ to look at the reflection as ☺ plays. Though ☺ might not realise who it is, this can encourage him or her to repeat simple play patterns.

Teach a simple 'my turn, your turn' game by handing over a toy and then holding out your hand for ☺ to pass it back. Repeat for several turns, keeping it fun.

Learn when to stand back and allow the baby time and space to explore a new plaything. This might be the time when they begin to repeat simple patterns and actions.

Select toys and playthings that are motivating and exciting when you repeat actions (for example musical stacking toys, activity centres or posting boxes that also make a noise).

When ☺ begins to repeat sounds such as 'bu-bu', lean close and echo back, making the string of sounds even longer: 'bu-bu-bu-bu'.

Follow the same routines and patterns by having set times for meals and snacks.

When you notice ☺ shaking a rattle or patting a teddy, gently take ☺'s hand and repeat the action a few times as you smile and encourage him or her.

Always approach from the front and say what you are going to do before, for example, wiping a baby's face with a cloth. This makes care routines more predictable and shows that communication follows a certain pattern.

Dip in

Play plan: Body talk

Area of Learning: CD   Focus: Expressing and Communicating Ideas   Individual target: Adopt body language to represent happy/grumpy/sad

Name: ....   Key person: ....

Help ☺ to interpret how other children are thinking and feeling from the way their faces look, the way they move, and the way they act.

Have fun with ☺ in front of a mirror, acting out different emotions. Use this time to talk naturally about feelings and to introduce some of the vocabulary of emotions.

Teach ☺ how to work out when and how someone can be interrupted. Teach 'excuse me', linking this to the skill of 'catching someone's eye' as well – so that it is not simply spoken 'at' someone.

Help the children to make their own set of photographs showing different emotions, and use these to help ☺ recognise feelings in others.

Help ☺ to make links between what other people appear to be feeling (from their body language, actions or voices) with what ☺ might do to help (cheer them up, come back later and so on).

Adopt a certain body position and expression in group time and ask the children to guess how you are feeling today.

Encourage ☺ to teach this same skill to a puppet in order to consolidate what has been learned.

Practise how close to stand when you are speaking to someone. When do you have to shout? When do you have to whisper?

Dip in

Play plan: Music all around

Name: ....

Key person: ....

Area of Learning: CD **Focus: Expressing and Communicating Ideas** **Individual target: Willing to express myself through music**

Set up a quiet area for ☺ to withdraw to if feeling overloaded and stressed. Play calming music and use soft surfaces, a favourite plaything or picture books to calm and soothe.

Play musical tapes and CDs at the end of your music time for the children to express themselves with rattles, shakers, drums and percussion.

Sing a regular song at transition times, such as 'Good morning everybody' or 'Time to say goodbye'. Encourage ☺ to express hello/goodbye.

Make music an integral part of your session. Use songs to signal routines such as 'Now it's time to have our drink' (to the tune of 'Girls and boys come out to play'). Ask ☺ what will happen next.

Use music to create different moods and atmospheres and try talking about how it makes you want to move. Experiment with different ways of expressing yourselves.

Plan a regular music circle time for all the children – to encourage musical expression, looking, listening and language skills. See page 8 for a reference to 'Music Makers'.

Select a range of diverse musical genres and styles to move to. Balance strongly rhythmical pieces with gentle, soothing ones. Celebrate and encourage all signs of expression from ☺, whether or not ☺ uses language.

Use music in wide open spaces as well as in small groups and circles. This way, ☺ might express himself/herself more freely. Share and celebrate any signs of joie-de-vivre!

Play plan: Keeping calm

Area of Learning: CD   Focus: Expressing and Communicating Ideas

Name: ....   Key person: ....

Individual target: Assert myself appropriately to other children

1 First make a detailed observation of how ☺ asserts himself/herself at present. Use the observation sheet on page 89.

2 Analyse your findings; what is ☺'s pattern? Some children assert themselves appropriately and join in well socially, some are too blunt, some are too passive and some get angry easily and are aggressive.

3 Decide on a target for ☺ – it might be that ☺ becomes more assertive, less aggressive or (for an older child) more tactful. Make a child-friendly statement, such as: '☺ will stay calm when another child wants to play.'

4 Use puppets to act out a few situations which show different reactions. For example, perhaps one puppet snatches another's favourite toy. What happens if the first puppet does nothing/fights back/asks the other to share?

5 Now try this out with the puppets. One puppet has been waiting patiently in a queue. Another pushes right in front. What might happen next? Talk about different possibilities.

6 Talk about good things that ☺ can learn to do: listening to others; not using an angry voice; telling people how you are feeling; asking nicely and calmly for things; working out how others are feeling.

7 Spot times when ☺ is behaving in this way and praise warmly and specifically ('I saw you asking Jamie nicely for the train – well done!').

8 If situations go awry, wait till ☺ is calm and use the puppets again to talk about different ways of reacting.

Sequential

Play plan: Topic talk

Area of Learning: CD

Focus: Expressing and Communicating Ideas

Name: ....

Key person: ....

Individual target: Gauge what the listener already knows when discussing topics

1 Observe the way that ☺ shares a topic of interest. Be aware of whether ☺ talks non-stop about favourite subjects. Would people who don't know ☺ understand what ☺ was saying? Perhaps it's time to target this.

2 Pretend you do not know what ☺ is talking about. Interrupt with a hand signal and a question, ☺, what are we talking about? – Thank you. Now tell me.'

3 In time, you can simply use the hand signal and ☺ will learn to pause in mid-flow and cue you in to the topic under discussion.

4 Continue to use interested questions to help ☺ to tell you the context. When did it happen? Who said that? What else happened? What happened next?

5 Set up a situation with two puppets in which your puppet knows something interesting and the other puppet has to guess what it is.

6 Set up talking times with adults who do not know ☺. Help ☺ to explain something interesting or new to them. Make sure the adults ask questions if they cannot follow what is said.

7 Look out for situations when ☺ needs help to tune in to what other children might be thinking or feeling. Praise specifically when you spot ☺ making use of what has been learned.

8 Help ☺ to prepare a little talk on a favourite topic for group time. Help ☺ work out what the children need to know. Help ☺ to choose props and talk about why these are helpful.

Sequential

Play plan: Planning Ahead

Name: ....

Area of Learning: CD   Focus: Expressing and Communicating Ideas

Individual target: Develop my ideas in the light of what we have talked about

Key person: ....

1
Use a plan/do/review format to encourage ☺ to plan ahead and talk about how an activity went.

2
Talk about how ☺ might like to try an activity again, but this time slightly differently. Show as well as tell, then step back to allow ☺ to follow through the ideas you have hatched together.

3
Now repeat the process using talk only. See if ☺ can try out the ideas (straight away, so that no long-term memory is required) without the aid of a visual demonstration too.

4
Now try to plan what ☺ might do the next day. This time, ☺ has to remember what you have talked about as well as retaining the ideas until the next day. Provide lots of support and reminders.

5
Use photographs of ☺'s creative activities and use these to talk about what ☺ would like to do in the next session.

6
Encourage ☺ to support a younger child in a creative activity.

7
Collate photographs of ☺'s creations and activities and ask ☺ to dictate a few words to explain what was happening. Adapt the language if you need to correct it and read back the correct version.

8
Think of a long-term project that ☺ might develop over several days. Ask ☺ to talk to you regularly about ☺'s ideas and creations (for example, planning a playground in a shoe box for a mouse family).

Developing Imagination and Imaginative Play

CD

Imaginative play is enriched and extended through words and language and this is where children with speech and language difficulties may need your additional support.

▲ ● ■ Links to Area of Learning

All children start to develop imagination by pretending that one object represents another and by replaying familiar roles and sequences of actions. They begin to notice what adults do, imitating what is observed and then doing it spontaneously when the adult is not there. They start to use one object to represent another even if the objects have very few characteristics in common. They also use available resources to create props to support their role play and begin to string more and more sequences of actions together. In these respects, children with speech and language difficulties may be no different to other children. However, when it comes to developing more imaginative and creative ways of playing, children with these difficulties sometimes face a barrier because they lack flexible ways of understanding and using language. They might find it easier to talk about the 'here and now' and the concrete rather than to use language to describe the imaginary and the abstract.

When children develop their role-play into more complex sequences of actions and roles, they often use words and language to mediate and regulate their play. They 'talk themselves through' what they are doing and also talk with their friends. In this way, their language helps them to develop ever more complex and imaginative ways of playing. Without the fluent use of language, children's repertoires of play may remain rather stereotyped and restricted. Once more confident and proficient in using language, children find it much easier to make links between their own first-hand experiences and their imaginative play. They start to enjoy stories based on themselves and people and places they know and also to 'lose themselves' in imaginative stories and rhymes. This makes them more likely to introduce a story line into their own play.

Improving language and communication skills allows them to play alongside others and share the game or activity, developing their imaginative ideas and learning from each other. They begin to play cooperatively with others and to 'think outside the box', thinking creatively in order to develop new ways of solving problems or developing their ideas. All this helps the children to achieve the Early Learning Goal of using their imagination in art and design, music, dance, imaginative and role-play and stories. If you can understand the barriers that children with speech and language difficulties might face during imaginative play, you can tune in to their needs more closely and provide additional support, using the activity ideas in this section.

▲ ● ■ Assessment records

You will find an assessment record on the next two pages for working out which skills and competencies the child has already acquired. As a starting point, look out for and work on behaviours that are sometimes, but not always, demonstrated.

Assessment sheet: Developing Imagination and Imaginative Play

Name:.............. Key person:..............

Communication, Language and Literacy

Creative Development: Developing Imagination and Imaginative Play

enter date observed

Development matters	What I do now	Never	Sometimes	Always
Pretending to hide	Watch 'peep-bo' with interest			
	Begin to anticipate during 'peep-bo'			
	Remove cloth from faces*			
	Play with a blanket			
	Play hide and seek			
Learning to imitate	Copy simple actions			
	Copy expressions			
	Copy words*			
	Copy simple role-play			
This will do for that	Use my favourite toy for a new purpose			
	Use a similar object to represent another (such as a toy cat as a cat)			
	Use a less obvious object to represent another (such as a brick as a plane)*			
Using props	Use my favourite plaything as a prop			
	Will accept a new prop from someone else			
	Use an obvious prop when role playing (such as a hat)			
	Dress up with support			
	Act out simple sequence with a prop (such as making the tea)			

Personal stories	Ask you for props to support my role play					
	Explain what I need to support my role play					
	Enjoy photographs of family and friends*					
	Settle down to look through a personal story book					
	Listen to narratives about myself with interest (no pictures)					
	Tell you what has happened to me					
	Invent a story about what might happen next					
Role playing alongside others	Watch others and put myself into a similar role					
	Follow the role-play of others and join in					
	Talk to other children as I play					
	Use different voices to support my role play*					
Invent imaginary ways of talking	Play imaginatively in a group					
	Express what I would like to play at					
	Negotiate roles with others					
	Bring new ideas into the play					
	Use language to share new ideas as I play*					

Early Learning Goals:

Use their imagination in art and design, music, dance, imaginative and role play and stories.

▲ ● ■ Look, listen and note

Here are some things to focus on especially when observing the imaginative play of children who have speech and language difficulties.

• In the early stages, note whether the child vocalises to attract your attention when pretending to hide or playing 'peep-bo'.

• Look out for and note down the first time an object triggers role play in a child – for example picking up a piece of wood that looks like a car and moving it along the table top. What noises, sounds or words does the child make to accompany this?

• Spend some time simply watching the child play. Can you see occasions when the child switches from real life to imaginary play? When did this happen? Again, did the child use language as well?

• Note the first few times that a child shares imaginary play with other children. How did this happen? Did the other child take the lead? Was language used or simply imitation? Did the play between them develop cooperatively?

• Observe incidences where the child moved from role play (copying well-known sequences of actions from the child's experience) to imaginary play (developing new and imaginary ways of playing and being). What props, other children or previous experiences made this most likely to take place?

▲ ● ■ Effective practice

• Use your own voice in a constant manner when playing hide and seek and 'peep-bo'. Demonstrate that language keeps you both in touch with each other.

• Exaggerate your facial expressions and tone of voice when telling stories and rhymes.

• Use themed areas (such as the home corner) for the child to practise and rehearse new roles (such as making the dinner) with your individual help and then introduce other children into the game to share this new way of playing.

• At first, suggest real props and then model how even unlikely objects can be used to pretend they are something else. Talk about why the prop is a good one.

• Use one-to-one or small groups to introduce new ways of playing imaginatively and model the language that might be used. Stand back and allow the child to enjoy and rehearse these new play repertoires with other children.

• Use pictures and story books to provide ideas for imaginative play. Talk about them, adapting your language to the child's level of understanding and expression.

• If a child has little experience of imaginary play, start by pairing that child up with another child who is a good role model for speech and language.

• Introduce vocabulary and words to support the child's play and revisit these new words later to consolidate them. Help the child to generalise them to other situations.

▲ ● ■ How to use the play plans

On pages 79–84 you will find six play plans for those skills marked with an asterisk on the assessment sheets on pages 76 and 77. Each play plan contains eight interventions that you could try. There are two blank spaces to add your own personalised interventions onto each play plan.

Dip in

Play plan: Now you see me...

Name: ....

Key person: ....

Area of Learning: CD   Focus: Developing imagination

Individual target: Remove cloth from faces

Play a 'peep-bo' game in a group. As you move to each baby, sing (for example) 'Amy-Lou, Amy-Lou! Where are you?' Then, as you withdraw the cloth, 'Here she is, here she is, how do you do?'

Place a cloth over a favourite toy and show ☺ how to draw the cloth away as you say, 'There it is!'

Place a scarf over your own face and keep calling ☺'s name until ☺ helps you pull it away.

Play a hide and seek game with each other, encouraging ☺ to call for you until you find ☺ again beneath the cloth or blanket.

Place a cloth over Teddy's eyes and call, 'Teddy! Where are you?' as you draw it away again. Share a chuckle as Teddy reappears.

Place a light chiffon scarf over ☺'s face and share the fun as you encourage ☺ to draw it off. Make a big fuss of ☺.

For children at risk of language delay, always accompany your game with words and vocalisations. Hide your face with a cloth and use your voice to hold ☺'s attention until you reappear with a smile and a greeting.

Use a large sheet to take it in turns to hide under. Keep calling, '☺ where are you?' until ☺ vocalises to you. Pretend that you simply cannot see ☺ until you hear that voice!

Dip in

Play plan: Fun to copy

Area of Learning: CD

Name: ....

Key person: ....

Focus: Developing imagination

Individual target: Copy words

When you teach ☺ a new word, make sure that ☺ can already say all the sounds involved and then spend a little time one-to-one or in a small group, listening and copying.

Adapt 'Old Macdonald' to include some speech sounds such as *baa, moo, la la, buzz, woof, grrr,* and so on.

Sing 'Old Macdonald Had a Farm' and encourage ☺ to join in 'E-I-E-I-O'. These sounds are easy to make yet involve stringing together a sequence.

Play a copying game with a small group of children and a mirror. Copy each other's face movements, sounds and also words.

Some children are more likely to copy words if they are accompanied by a sign. See pages 8 and 95 for some resources and contacts for signing, or speak with any speech and language therapist involved.

Start by helping ☺ to copy sounds. Gather several toy animals or pictures of animals. As you look at each one, encourage ☺ to copy the animal sounds.

Play games that involve clever mouth movements like sucking through a straw, blowing a feather across a table, licking honey from around your mouth, blowing ink pictures with a straw, and so on.

Ask ☺ to teach the new word that ☺ has just learned to a puppet or soft toy.

Encourage ☺ to watch your whole face and sit somewhere quiet so ☺ can hear the sounds.

Play plan: Take one block

Name: ....

Key person: ....

Area of Learning: CD   **Focus:** Developing imagination   **Individual target:** Use a less obvious object to represent another

Give ☺ and friends a block to serve as a prop as you sing, 'This is the way we brush our hair/drive a car/hammer a nail' (and so on), turning the block into many different roles.

Make a plan of your local area and find everyday objects to represent different buildings – 'This rubber can be your house. This paper can be the park...' And so on.

Collect interesting and safe natural objects such as driftwood and pine cones. Add them to your prop box so that each thing can be pretended into different functions.

Use different objects for a range of activities, such as counting with pebbles or shells or painting with twigs.

Move in to play alongside ☺ from time to time and make suggestions for props – 'Look – this pencil could be your wand!' Mime the action at the same time.

Model to ☺ how you can pretend a block becomes different things. Make it into a car together by moving it along and making sounds. Try combing your hair with it. Share the fun.

Offer the children a 'treasure bag' and ask them to go on a pirate trek collecting 'treasure' from your everyday objects. As you open the bag, go into role, 'Arr! A gold cup we have here...'.

Play a guessing game – hold up a pebble and describe what you are pretending it to be: 'I am round all over and children throw me and kick me.' Mime the action for ☺ as well.

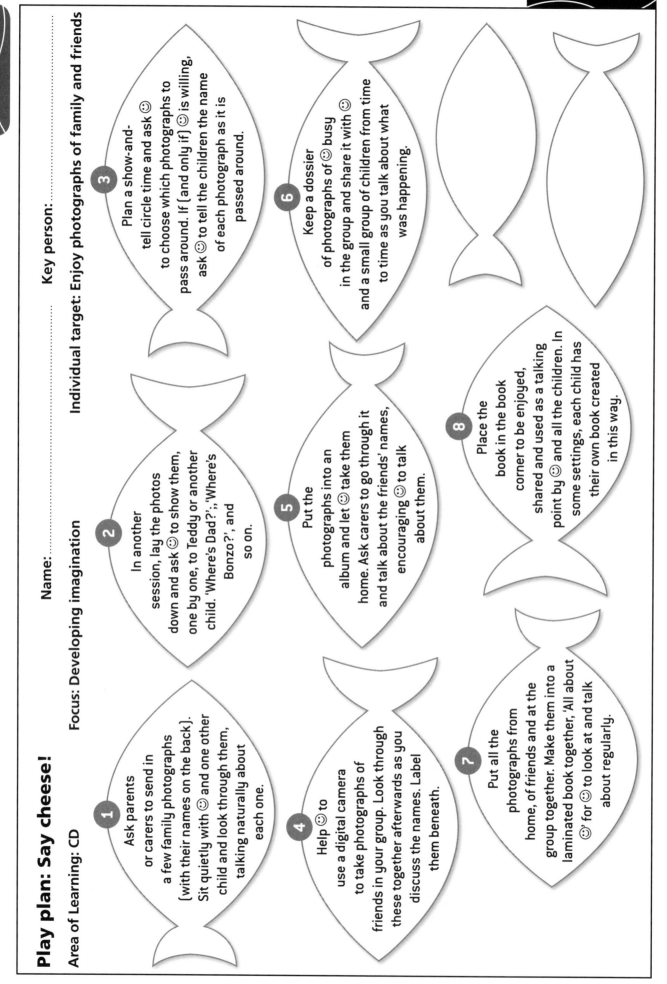

Sequential

Play plan: Say cheese!

Area of Learning: CD

Focus: Developing imagination

Name: ....

Key person: ....

Individual target: Enjoy photographs of family and friends

1 Ask parents or carers to send in a few family photographs (with their names on the back). Sit quietly with ☺ and one other child and look through them, talking naturally about each one.

2 In another session, lay the photos down and ask ☺ to show them, one by one, to Teddy or another child. 'Where's Dad?'; 'Where's Bonzo?', and so on.

3 Plan a show-and-tell circle time and ask ☺ to choose which photographs to pass around. If (and only if) ☺ is willing, ask ☺ to tell the children the name of each photograph as it is passed around.

4 Help ☺ to use a digital camera to take photographs of friends in your group. Look through these together afterwards as you discuss the names. Label them beneath.

5 Put the photographs into an album and let ☺ take them home. Ask carers to go through it and talk about the friends' names, encouraging ☺ to talk about them.

6 Keep a dossier of photographs of ☺ busy in the group and share it with ☺ and a small group of children from time to time as you talk about what was happening.

7 Put all the photographs from home, of friends and at the group together. Make them into a laminated book together, 'All about ☺' for ☺ to look at and talk about regularly.

8 Place the book in the book corner to be enjoyed, shared and used as a talking point by ☺ and all the children. In some settings, each child has their own book created in this way.

Dip in

Play plan: Various voices

Name: .... Key person: ....

Area of Learning: CD Focus: Developing imagination Individual target: Use different voices to support my role play

Place a collection of toy animals in a bag and draw them out, one by one. Ask: 'If they could talk, what would they sound like? Try saying 'Hello everyone' in that voice!'

Invite ☺ and friends to make a recording of their imaginary game for the other children to listen to. Help them to discover that using different voices makes it more interesting to listen to.

Try some group drama in which you all go somewhere in your imaginations (led by the children) – such as a trip on a magic carpet. Use different voices to represent the characters that you choose together.

Collect a series of magnificent dressing-up hats and then play with trying them on and trying different voices to go with them.

Give puppets different personae and characteristics – the kind one, the fierce one, the happy one, and so on. Experiment with different tones of voice as you make them speak and interact together.

If invited, join in with ☺'s role play and use your own voice to model variations on how the characters speak. Stand back again and hear whether your new ideas are taken up and developed.

Exaggerate your own tones of voice when telling stories and rhymes. Ask the children how they think the character is feeling. Why do they think the character feels like that?

Try the voices rhyme: you say (for example), 'Have you got your MONSTER voices?' and the children reply [loudly and fiercely], 'YES WE HAVE!'. Introduce squeaky/growly/robot/filmstar voices and so on.

Dip in

Play plan: Good ideas

Name: .... Key person: ....

Area of Learning: CD   Focus: Developing imagination   Individual target: Use language to share new ideas as I play

Set up a pirate game. Ask ☺ to explain to another child where some treasure is hidden in another room or outside.

Talk about your plans for the day at group time and encourage ☺ to contribute some ideas. At first, help ☺ to accompany this with props, such as something made yesterday.

Start a 'good ideas' scrapbook or picture gallery with photographs of the children and their own words as dictated to you beneath.

Ask ☺ to work with a younger child on a collage and ask ☺ to give the other child some good ideas.

As ☺ plays naturally, move in occasionally to pose questions and problems; 'I wonder what would happen if...' or 'Oh no – another lion has come too!' Use language that ☺ can understand and build on.

Play with ☺ one-to-one as you work out together how to make something. Model the language as well as the actions. Then ask ☺ to help a group of children to do this, using ☺'s ideas.

Sit in a small circle and invent an adventure story, each child in turn adding the next idea to the plot.

Introduce a sad puppet who feels that he never has a good idea. Ask ☺ to help it to think of something new and exciting to do in the group and tell the others.

Play plan: Copy this blank play plan so that you can make your own plan.

Name: ....

Area of Learning: ....

Key person: ....

Individual target: ....

Focus: ....

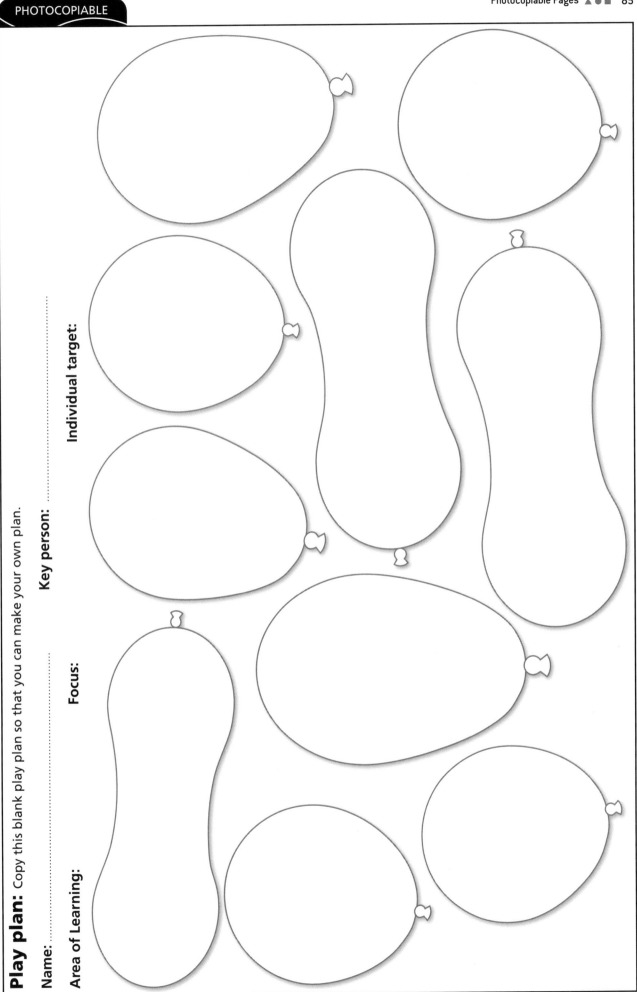

Monitoring sheet Copy this sheet and use it to monitor how your play plans went.

Name: .... **Key person:** ....

Area of Learning: .... **Focus:** ....

Individual target: ....

What we did	How it worked	Next steps

Home plan Copy this sheet and use it to share your activities at home.

Name: .... **Key person:** ....

Area of Learning: .... **Focus:** ....

This week we are helping .... **to:** ....

It would be really helpful if you could try this at home:

....

How did .... **get on:** ....

Summary sheet

Copy this sheet and use it as a summary of your work for the next review meeting.

Name: ....

Focus: ....

Individual target: ....

Area of Learning: ....

Key person: ....

Date: ....

Outcome	Summary of progress	Challenges to be met	Help from home	Next steps

Signed: ....

Date: ....

■SCHOLASTIC

www.scholastic.co.uk

Observation sheet
Use this sheet to record examples of the child's speech, language and communication in different situations.

Name of child: ....

Date	What I noticed the child do/say	What else was going on at a the time	Ideas for support and progress	Observer

Baby Talk
How to communicate with your baby

The first few months

• Your baby will begin to communicate to you by crying. This is normal and helps you know when your baby needs feeding, changing, putting down for a rest or comforting. After a week or two you will probably begin to recognise the different cries and know how to go about your daily activities.

• Sing to your baby either on your lap or when your baby is going to sleep.

• Limit the length of time that your baby spends in front of a TV.

• When your baby is awake, sit or lie your baby where he or she can watch you.

Older babies

• Pause when you talk to your baby and allow your baby time to make sounds back to you.

• Sit your baby on your knee facing you as you sing songs and say action rhymes together. Hold your baby's attention with your facial expressions and by sharing fun together.

• Read your baby a short story and look at the pictures. Your baby does not understand yet but will enjoy sharing this with you.

• Talk about things you see as you go out with the buggy.

• Enjoy 'peep-bo' games together.

• Name familiar objects around your baby. Though your baby cannot speak yet, this will help to develop understanding later on.

• When your baby starts to talk, try not to put him or her off by asking too many questions. Instead, talk together naturally about what is going on.

■SCHOLASTIC
www.scholastic.co.uk

The action word song

Share this action rhyme together in a small group or during circle time. Build in plenty of different action words. Pause dramatically at the 'STOP!' to encourage everyone to look and listen together. This rhyme is really successful with very young children.

We clap and we clap and we STOP!

We clap and we clap and we STOP!

We clap and we clap and we clap and we clap

We clap and we clap and we STOP!

We walk and we walk and we STOP!

We walk and we walk and we STOP!

We walk and we walk and we walk and we walk

We walk and we walk and we STOP!

We wriggle and wriggle and STOP!

We wriggle and wriggle and STOP!

We wriggle and wriggle and wriggle and wriggle

We wriggle and wriggle and STOP!

Hannah Mortimer

Bumpy speech

Many children go through a patch of 'bumpy' speech where they might stammer or stutter. Share this handout with colleagues and families so that you can help the chihldren become more fluent.

Top tips for helping bumpy speakers

• Slow down your pace of talking with the child. Keep your language simple and uncomplicated.

• Try to give the child your full attention when the child is talking to you.

• Do not interrupt the child as you listen.

• Cut down direct questions or asking the child to say something in front of other people. Talk and chatter naturally together instead so that the child feels relaxed about using language.

• Do not correct words or phrases that are wrongly said but simply echo back what you think the child was trying to say and then respond.

• Always make sure that a child knows what is expected by having clear rules and routines.

• Plan some activities where the child is most likely to feel relaxed and likely to want to talk.

• If a child speaks far too quickly, slow your own talk down – this often helps them to slow down as well (and is more effective than nagging!).

• Keep your eye contact even if a child's speech is very bumpy – this shows that you are interested in what they have to say.

• Never finish a word that a child is trying to say, even if it is hard for them to say.

• Look for chances to speak with the child in a relaxed one-to-one or small-group situation and make this a priority each day.

• Make sure that the child is praised frequently and has plenty of chances to feel successful and confident each day.

Is your child's speech hard to understand?

Here is what you can do to help.

• Little children start to learn the sounds they will use when speaking long before they learn to speak proper words. Sometimes some sounds do not get learned and this makes their words unclear later on.

• Try to remain patient. Some words and sounds are hard for a young child to make and this can be frustrating for both of you.

• Don't keep correcting your child – this can put a child off trying to speak.

• Instead, model correctly what you think your child was trying to say, emphasising the word that was difficult to say. For example, if your child says, 'Want dooz on!', you could say, 'Yes, we'll put your shoes on'.

• Play it again: if you cannot understand what your child is saying, explain that you did not hear properly and ask for a repeat.

• Ask your child to show you what they want or what they are talking about as well as telling you.

• Play with sounds. Try action rhymes (such as 'Old Macdonald Had a Farm') and talk about animal sounds (such as *baa, moo, buzz, woof, grrr* and so on).

• Collect toys that have certain sounds attached to them (such as a car that goes brmm brmm). Pull these out of a bag, one at a time, as you say the sound and guess what is next.

• Some children whose speech is very unclear find it helpful to learn some signs. These actually help the words become clearer as they help you understand what your child is trying to say and therefore encourage language. A speech and language therapist might be able to advise you.

Supportive play

Share this handout with parents and carers for children who need to build their confidence as well as their language skills.

• Set a specific time for ten minutes supportive play per day.

• Ask your child to decide what you want to do together (within reason). If in doubt, offer choices from a box or suitcase of playthings that you have kept specially.

• Agree on an activity or game.

• Participate wholeheartedly, following your child's lead.

• Talk simply about what your child is doing to show that you are paying full attention ('I see you are …', 'I wonder what will happen when …').

• Say things such as 'I like it when you …' to show that you value his or her play.

• Praise your child repeatedly. Do not use 'No…' statements and do not nag or criticise.

• Laugh and share a giggle together through physical play and hugs.

• Finish by talking simply about what you have done together.

Resources

Books for adults

Many of the clearest books are written for parents and carers yet are also excellent introductions for early years' practitioners.

• *Communicating Matters* – training materials published by Sure Start, DfES and Primary National Strategy (2005). Available through the DfES Orderline at dfes@prolog.uk.com or Tel: 0845 60 22 260 (Ref: 1771 to 1779-2005DOC-EN)

• *Developing early intervention/support services for deaf children and their families* (for Local Authorities, teachers of the deaf and others working with very young deaf children). From DfES Publications (Tel: 0845 602 2260. Reference number: LEA/ 0068/2003)

• *Information for parents – Speech and language Difficulties.* Available from DfES Publications. Tel 0845 602 2260 or e-mail dfes@prolog.uk.com (Ref: PPMRP/D32/ 21154/1106/14)

• *Music Makers: Music circle times to include everyone* by Hannah Mortimer (QEd) www.qed.uk.com

• *It Takes Two to Talk – a practical guide for parents of children with language delays* by Jan Pepper and Elaine Weitzman. A Hanen Centre publication available through Winslow Press, Tel: 01869 244644.

• *Working with Children with Specific Learning Difficulties in the Early Years* by Dorothy Smith (QEd) www.qed.uk.com

• *Learning Language and Loving It: A Guide to Promoting Children's Social, Language, and Literacy Development in Early Childhood Settings* (Second Edition, Weitzman and Greenberg, 2002) avaialble from the Hanen Centre www.hanen.org

• Sure Start – *Supporting families that have children with special needs and disabilities* (guidance for Sure Start local programmes but also suitable also for children's centres and individual settings). www.surestart.gov.uk

• *Baby Talk – strengthening your child's ability to listen, understand and communicate* by Sally Ward (Century Publishing)

Resources

• Acorn Educational Ltd: 32 Queen Eleanor Road, Geddington, Kettering, Northants NN14 1AY (equipment and resources including special needs).

• Ann Arbor Publishers, PO Box 1, Belford, Northumberland NE70 7JK (books, assessment and learning resources that support learning disabilities).

• 'Solutions for Pupils with Special Needs' resource catalogue, Don Johnston Special Needs, 18/19 Clarendon Court, Calver Road, Winwick Quay, Warrington WA2 8QP. www.donjohnston.com

• Jolly Learning Ltd (information on Jolly Phonics), Tailours House, High Road, Chigwell, Essex IG7 6DL. www.jollylearning.co.uk

• LDA Primary and Special Needs, Duke Street, Wisbech, Cambridgeshire PE13 2AE. Tel: 01945 463441.

• NferNelson produce a Specialist Assessment Catalogue. Tel: 0845 602 1937 www.nfer-nelson.co.uk

• The Psychological Corporation produces a catalogue of Educational assessment and intervention resources. Tel: 01865 888188 www.tpc-international.com

• Step by step – toys and equipment for all special needs. Tel: 0845 3001089

• Winslow's Education and Special Needs catalogue (good resources for language support). Tel: 0845 921 1777 email: sales@winslow-cat.com

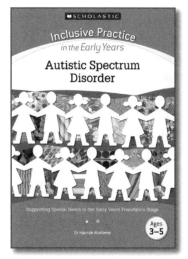
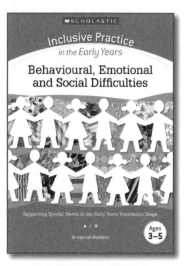
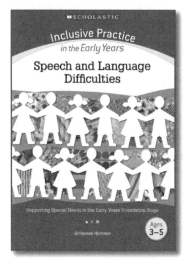